Y0-AGT-176

As Luther Taught the Word of Truth

Devotions on the Small Catechism

Richard E. Lauersdorf

Northwestern Publishing House
Milwaukee, Wisconsin

Second printing, 2004

All Scripture quotations, unless otherwise indicated, are taken from the HOLY BIBLE, NEW INTERNATIONAL VERSION®. NIV®. Copyright © 1973, 1978, 1984 by International Bible Society. Used by permission of Zondervan Publishing House. All rights reserved.

The "NIV" and "New International Version" trademarks are registered in the United States Patent and Trademark Office by International Bible Society. Use of either trademark requires the permission of International Bible Society.

All rights reserved. No part of this publication may be reproduced, stored in a retrieval system, or transmitted in any form or by any means—electronic, mechanical, photocopying, recording, or otherwise—except for brief quotations in reviews, without prior permission from the publisher.

Library of Congress Control Number 2002100790
Northwestern Publishing House
1250 N. 113th St., Milwaukee, WI 53226-3284
© 2002 by Northwestern Publishing House
Published 2002
Printed in the United States of America
ISBN 0-8100-1457-2

Contents

Preface

When's the last time you reached for Luther's Small Catechism? For many of us, that was the book of instruction in our youth, the first summary of the important truths of God's Word we ever studied.

Those of us who have returned to the Small Catechism over the years have found it ever more valuable. Simply and positively this little volume summarizes the precious truths of Holy Scripture in language that we can understand and use. Its emphasis on the supremacy of Christ and his Word focuses our attention where it ought to be. Regardless of our age, each one of us can benefit by remaining a child and pupil of the Small Catechism.

Its author, Dr. Martin Luther, wrote: "It is highly profitable and fruitful daily to read it and make it the subject of meditation and conversation. In such reading, conversation and meditation," he continued, "the Holy Spirit is present and bestows ever new and greater light and fervor so that day by day we relish and appreciate the Catechism more greatly" (Tappert, *Book of Concord*, page 359).

May the Lord in his grace use these meditations based on Luther's Small Catechism to deepen our understanding and appreciation of the Word of Truth as Luther taught us in our youth.

The First Article of the Apostles' Creed

I believe in God the Father almighty, maker of heaven and earth.

What does this mean?

I believe that God created me and all that exists, that he gave me my body and soul, eyes, ears, and all my members, my mind and all my abilities.

And I believe that God still preserves me by richly and daily providing clothing and shoes, food and drink, property and home, spouse and children, land, cattle, and all I own, and all I need to keep my body and life. God also preserves me by defending me against all danger, guarding and protecting me from all evil. All this God does only because he is my good and merciful Father in heaven, and not because I have earned or deserved it. For all this I ought to thank and praise, to serve and obey him.

This is most certainly true.

The First Article

"I believe . . ."

All of us do it several times each month. At the appropriate point in the service, the worship leader announces, "Let us join in confessing our faith in the words of the Apostles' Creed," and we begin our response with these two words: "I believe." But what's all involved in that brief statement?

A personal word

Being alone is not something most people enjoy. Just watch someone eating alone in a restaurant or standing apart on a school playground. By nature we are gregarious people; we want to be with others. Even in a worship service, there's meaning to being surrounded by people hearing the same truths and sending the same praises and prayers heavenward as we do.

Yet when it comes to what is believed, no "we" or "they" will do. My spouse, who walks beside me as life's partner, can't speak as my proxy. My parents, who gave me life, can't be my surrogate. I must answer for myself. That's the way God in his wisdom designed it. A relationship with him is always personal.

The apostle named Thomas finally learned that lesson. The others had told him what they had seen and believed on Easter. One week later, with the risen Savior standing before him and reaching out with nail-pierced hands just for him, Thomas confessed, "*My* Lord and *my*

God!" (John 20:28). Paul learned that lesson too. Sought out by God's grace on the Damascus road, schooled deeply in God's Word, sent to speak the Word's central message of salvation in Christ Jesus, Paul never stopped marveling, "I live by faith in the Son of God, who loved *me* and gave himself for *me*" (Galatians 2:20).

What a miracle that I can join Thomas and Paul in speaking so personally about the Lord. This series of devotions on Luther's Small Catechism purposely begins with the Creed and not with the Ten Commandments. Before we discuss what God wants us to do for him, we need to look at what he has done for us. The Creed is pure gospel, setting forth the marvelous things the triune God, in his mercy and grace, has done for us. Included in this list, equally high on the list, is the faith he has worked in my heart. The personal word *I* with which we begin the Creed is at the same time also a thankful word. With thanksgiving I declare, "*I* believe."

A confident word

"I" what? "Believe," you say? Yes, "believe." But what does that mean? Am I saying that I *know* something about God? That I *acknowledge* he has done some great things? Or is it more than that?

Our youngest child took her first steps in a shoe store in Milwaukee. I can still see her in that aisle, little arms stretched out confidently to me as she all at once launched forth from the protective grip of her mother's hands. Of course, she *knew* us as her father and mother. Of course, she *knew* that we would take care of her, changing her diapers and giving her that midnight feeding. But it was more than knowing us and acknowledging our care that launched her on those first steps. It was the *trust* that we would catch her and not let her pudgy nose be flattened on the aisle floor. She confidently bet her first steps on us.

Isn't that what I mean when I confess, "I *believe*"? Like Noah swinging the hammer in building the ark for 120 years, it means "I am confident that what God says he will do." Like Abraham leaving his homeland for he knew not where, it means "I am confident that when God tells me to go, he will not only go with me but will even lead." Like Stephen facing death at the hands of the mob, it means "I am confident that when God calls me, he will carry me home."

One thing I do know—I'll always need more faith. On this side of heaven, my confidence in God will never be complete nor will my leaning on his promises ever be one hundred percent. But thank God that I know where to go. "Faith comes from hearing the message," he has told me through his apostle, "and the message is heard through the word of Christ" (Romans 10:17). To the Word I must go if I want to say with conviction, "I believe."

Prayer: Lord, for my faith I thank you alone. For its strengthening I trust you alone. Amen.

The First Article

"... in God the Father almighty ..."

How do I approach the One in whom I believe? Some of us have been approaching God for so long now that perhaps we don't even think about the how. Do I approach him sporadically like some stranger to whom I barely nod? Do I sidle up to him with a shiver, fearing his holy glance? Should I drape my arm around his shoulders like some old buddy with whom I feel on equal terms? Or can those familiar words, "I believe in God the Father almighty," teach me something about approaching God?

With reverence

I remember the first time I preached to a roomful of pastors. It was during my vicar year in Tucson. My mouth was dry as cotton; the words came slowly; and finally I was done. Afterwards, my supervising pastor commented, "Always remember that they put their shirts on the same way you do." His advice has helped me ever since, and I've passed it on to many a vicar and young pastor.

That's how one preaches to pastors. But how do I approach God? Must it not be with a sense of his greatness and my littleness? His majesty and my nothingness? His eternalness and my fleeting brevity? Yes, with all of the above. But even more than that, must it not be with an overwhelming sense of his complete holiness and my utter sinfulness. Like Simon Peter that day on the Lake of Gennesaret—overwhelmed not so much by the boat full of fish as by his soul full of iniquity—my only reaction can be, "Go away from me, Lord; I am a sinful man!" (Luke 5:8).

That's the holy God of whom I speak and whom I dare to approach. When I recognize this, I utter words such as "Be merciful to me," not because I ought to but because I have to. In his presence I can say nothing more. With empty hand and trembling heart, I approach the holy God.

With confidence

And yet I approach him with confidence, because I also know him as "the Father almighty." (The Apostles' Creed uses only these two words of him, so they must be important.) "Father," I call him, not because I have earned the right to do so but because he has given me this privilege. He's everyone's God—but not everyone's Father. There are many children in the world, but not all are *his* children. In his love, and entirely because of his grace, he has adopted me into his family of believers. I can call him "Father," because he first calls me "child." Try as I might, live as long as he lets me, I'll never exhaust the grace behind these words: "You are all sons of God through faith in Christ Jesus, for all of you who were baptized into Christ have clothed yourselves with Christ" (Galatians 3:26,27).

What confidence I have knowing God is my Father. Regardless of my circumstances and irrespective of my age, my Father's heart is there to hug me, his arms to help me, his ears to hear me, his eyes to behold me. To him I can go with confidence, and in his presence I can feel safe. This I believe because my Father has made and keeps it so.

Moreover, my Father is "almighty." Here's no well-intentioned but not always capable dad. For my Father "nothing is impossible," as Mary once was told (Luke 1:37). He who placed his eternal Son as a seed inside a virgin's womb can handle anything that might come my way. What burden is there that my almighty Father cannot lift it from my shoulders or strengthen my muscles so I can carry it. What so-called evil can come my way that his power, directed by his love, cannot make serve my good. Even life's greatest enemy, that monster called death, must throw in the towel when my almighty Father comes to carry my living soul home and on the last day to claim my lifeless clay. This I believe because my almighty Father has made and keeps it so.

How do I approach God? With reverence, of course, because he's the holy God. But even more so, with confidence, because he's my Father almighty.

Prayer: Father, thank you for making me your dear child through Christ Jesus. Help me trust your power and love to care for me as your very own. Amen.

The First Article

"... maker of heaven and earth ..."

"I have the answer. What's your question?" said the bumper sticker on the car ahead of me on the freeway. How typical of man to think he has the answer for everything—and as usual, his answers lie on the horizontal, not the vertical, plane, pointing not to God but only to himself. Ask about life's purpose and his answers point to his own pleasure or promotion. Ask about reaching eternity, and his answers involve his own sweating and striving. Ask about his origin—where he and all around him came from—and the answers still refuse to look up to the Almighty. But not so with those who by divine grace call God their "Father Almighty." For them there's marvelous meaning in the expression "Maker of heaven and earth."

My Father made it all

What an awesome sight! Flying the red-eye flight from Yaounde, Cameroon, Africa to Frankfurt, Germany, I woke at dawn from a fretful sleep just as we were over the Alps in Italy. Never will I forget the sight of those snowcapped peaks standing majestically in the sunshine above the clouds. I didn't sing it, but surely thought it: *How great thou art, my heavenly Father.*

What an awesome sight! In my wife's arms nestled our newly born daughter. In her little eight pounds were packed 206 bones and 639 muscles, a little heart that would beat 100,000 times a day on average, and tiny lungs that would breathe some 23,800 times a day for the rest of her life—not to mention a soul that was created to live forever and had already been paid for by the precious blood of Jesus. Again I didn't sing it, but surely thought it: *How great thou art, my heavenly Father.*

Not everyone could see what I was seeing. Only those to whom God has given the eyes of faith can see him in his creation. That's one of the wonderful things about being children of the Father in heaven. We see things as we have not seen them before. When we look at the heavens with their innumerable stars and grand galaxies, we see more than molecules of matter. When we look at our earth with its rich and varied resources, we see not an accidental mass molded by some "big bang" millions of years back in space but the work of God's hand. And when we look at man, for whom it was all made, we see not an evolving surprise still unfinished but the crown of God's creation. Behind all this, bigger than all this, beyond all this, is God the Father Almighty. My Father who made me and saved me, who loves me and will glorify me, is the Maker of heaven and earth.

My Father made it all for me

That's right, he *made it all for me.* "You made him ruler over the works of your hands; you put everything under his feet," David marvels in Psalm 8:6. Into the fantastic world God had created, he placed man. It was all his to discover and develop for his own good and God's glory. And so man has gone at it. He cuts deeply into the earth's crust and catapults miles into space. He cures diseases and comes up with ways to prevent them. He communicates via cyberspace and compresses widespread nations into a global society.

Yet something is radically wrong. Those who have eyes even half open recognize this troubling fact. He who was created to rule has let his scepter slip—as he now uses what the Creator made for him both to heal and to harm, both to build up and to tear down. Corrupted by sin, he pursues his own selfish interests and pins the medals of praise on his own chest. To and for himself he looks, not realizing how utterly our first parents' fall into sin has corrupted him.

And we? What do we see? How blessed we are to know that the Father Almighty not only planned his universe down to the smallest detail but also included in his eternal scheme the undoing of sin's damage. For me he has prepared total cleansing through his Son's precious blood. To me he has given a new heart, alive through faith. From me, his child, he now desires responsible use of what he has created for me. Before me he places the promise of a new heaven and new earth, untouched and unsullied by sin, where eternity will find me singing his praises.

All this I, as his child, find in that marvelous expression "Maker of heaven and earth."

Prayer: Almighty Father, accept our praise for the world into which you have placed us, and help us never to cease marveling at your wisdom and love behind it all. In Jesus' name. Amen.

The First Article

"I believe that God created me and all that exists, that he gave me my body and soul, eyes, ears, and all my members, my mind and all my abilities."

"Make sure you visit those parents in the maternity ward," a seasoned pastor sagely advised his younger colleagues. How near God appears when a new life is nestled in a mother's arms. How wondrous his workings appear in granting that miracle.

"Let us make man," the triune God said on the sixth day of creation. I am that man and so are you. The almighty Creator gave life to each of us as both a loving and a lasting gift.

A loving gift

"Body and soul" he made us. "Eyes, ears, and members" he gave us along with a "mind and abilities." So it was with our first parents, Adam and Eve, whom he made in most wondrous ways. So it is also with each of us, whom he has made through our parents in that wondrous way we call reproduction. Some label life only an accident, the haphazard result of parental union. Others lament life, complaining that they didn't choose to be born. Still others play loosely with life, snuffing it out either inside or outside the womb. But the fact remains. God the Father almighty created me and all that exists. My life is a loving gift from his hand, a gift to be treasured.

My life is a loving gift in other ways. Just look at the body he gave me to house my life. One summer while I was visiting my nephew in New York, I toured his place of work. With pride he showed me a huge computerized machine into which a flat sheet of metal was automatically fed. With much noise and back and forth motion and without a human hand touching it, a cut and punched light fixture form ready for wiring and flourescent bulbs came out of the other end of that machine. Tremendous? Absolutely! But nothing like my body. No machine can ever duplicate what God has programmed my body to do. Think of all that I can do at work or play with the arms and legs, hands and fingers, back and shoulders, skeletal form and nervous system God has given me.

Think also of how the body he gave me is able to ward off disease and repair itself when damaged. No machine from any century can do that. Think too of the computer the Creator has quartered in my cranium, a marvel that man will never be able to duplicate. Made of tissue and fed by the bloodstream just like the rest of my body, yet my brain controls it all. Not only does it react, but, unlike that of animals, it reasons and responds, enabling me to discover and control the world God has made for me.

Though the curse of sin has damaged and the course of time deteriorates what God gave me, whether eight days or 80 years old, we exclaim with David, "I praise you because I am fearfully and wonderfully made; your works are wonderful, I know that full well" (Psalm 139:14).

A lasting gift

"A gift that lasts forever," encouraged the billboard ad from the jewelry store at Christmastime. Diamonds, however, don't last forever. They can be lost or stolen. Death rips them off our finger or locks them with us in the casket. But the life God gives lasts forever.

Body and soul he gave Adam and Eve. Body and soul he also gave me—a body to house me while in this world and a soul that he intends to live with him forever. Through sin, Adam and Eve threw away for themselves and for all following generations the complete holiness and perfect knowledge that composed the divine image in which God had created them. By their sin they exchanged fellowship with God for fighting against God; following God's gracious will for flailing against it; blessed never-ending life with God for life with the devil—a life that they could only futilely hope would not last forever.

Thank God that in his love he also recreates me! Double blessings are mine as his child. He who made me in my mother's womb now remakes me in Christ. Through the Savior's payment for my sins and the Spirit's gift of faith, he refashions me, restoring in me his holy image that will be fully mine in heaven. In the resurrection, he has waiting for me a perfect body to replace the one laid low by death on earth. Just look at what he does for me that I can be the creation he intended when he first made man.

Prayer: For the life you have given us through creating and redeeming us, we thank you, Lord. Help us to live for you on earth until we live with you in heaven. Amen.

The First Article

"And I believe that God still preserves me . . ."

When we bought our house, the builder gave us a list of subcontractors who had worked on it. Why? We soon found out—of course after the warranty had expired—when we had to replace the programmable thermostat. The builder had built the house, but keeping it running was up to us. How different it is with our almighty Father, the divine builder of heaven and earth. What he created, he also preserves.

Only he can do it

Make no mistake about it. The Creator is still the owner. Wherever we look, we find his loving fingerprints. Our God is no absentee landlord who only sporadically visits to see how his tenants are doing and how his buildings are faring. He's no sideline spectator who once in a while drives by just out of curiosity. "By him all things were created . . . and in him all things hold together," Paul reminds us (Colossians 1:16,17). This is still *his world.* If it weren't, it would have long ago fallen into total ruin.

Sometimes we forget this important truth. After all, don't we cross the fields with the planter and later with the combine? Plant the flowers and pick the blossoms? Discover the medicines and dispense them by prescriptions? Build the hospitals and fund the research? Go to work and bring home the paycheck? Get the groceries and microwave the meals? Put up our dwellings and pay our mortgages? Put aside our savings and plan our retirements? Split atoms and soar into space? Invent computers and send e-mail messages? Where do we find God's fingerprints in all this? Only when the rain fails to fall and the seed shrivels, when the medicine doesn't work and the sickness worsens, when the job and the paycheck disappear, are we again reminded that this is not our world. It is still his, and he alone can keep it running.

And so he has been doing, not just for a year or two, a century or a half, a millenium past or present, but since the world began. And so he will until it ends. With our human minds, we can describe this gracious preservation of his creation by the Creator, but we can't make it happen. We toss around terms like the "laws of nature" to describe sunrise and sunset, seedtime and harvest, summer and winter, life and death—but behind it all stands the infinite wisdom of the Creator's planning and the inexhaustible reservoir of his power.

He does it for all

Jesus said it, and we know from observation that it's true. "He [the Father in heaven] causes his sun to rise on the evil and the good, and sends rain on the righteous and the unrighteous" (Matthew 5:45). Sometimes we wonder why. We might suggest that our Father tell the unworthy, "Name just one thing you have done for me that I should preserve you." That he tell the ungrateful, "Forget it, I'm through with you." That he tell the rebellious, "Go ahead, sink or swim on your own." But he doesn't. And we know why. It's for the same reason that he preserves each one of us. He grants and preserves life as a time of grace so that each individual might learn to know him as their Father and his Son as their only Savior.

Sometimes we wonder if he really does provide for all. Where is he? and what is he doing? we ask when confronted by the starving in far-off lands and by the abandoned and neglected in our homeland. So quickly we point the blaming finger at him when we should be pointing it at man whose selfishness and stubbornness dam up the sharing of the abundance received from God's preserving hand.

He does it for me

That's the main thought. *He does it for me.* Every day I need Jeremiah's reminder: "Because of the Lord's great love we are not consumed, for his compassions never fail. They are new every morning" (Lamentations 3:22,23). I've earned only his punishment, but he grants me continued breath and daily bread. I so often fail to see his providing hand, but it keeps on pouring out blessings in abundance. I neglect to offer him thanks and praise, but he doesn't decrease his largesse. Could it be that he who so lovingly sent Jesus to remove my sins wants me to survive until he takes me home to his glory? Oh, thank the Lord who preserves me until that eternal day.

Prayer: Lord, open our eyes to see your providing hand behind the world and us. Move us to be more grateful for what you give us daily. Amen.

The First Article

"... richly and daily providing clothing and shoes, food and drink, property and home, spouse and children, land, cattle, and all I own, and all I need to keep my body and life."

They hurried and scurried this way and that. I had just run over an ant hill with the lawnmower and was looking at the results. The sight made me wonder what we might look like from God's point of view on high. When God looks down from heaven, do we look like a bunch of ants scurrying and hurrying this way and that in our consternation and concern or like his children who know how well the heavenly Father takes care of us?

What he provides

Like some smorgasbord, Luther lays before us the many items that God provides richly and daily for our body and life. Though we no longer spin and sew clothing in our homes or crudely cobble shoes on homemade lasts, we wear such items daily. Though most of us no longer plant potatoes or squeeze the milk from a cow, we are happy to find such commodities in the supermarkets and on our tables. Though we no longer build homes from trees we have felled and logs we have split, a roof over our heads is still a necessity. Though many in the world have torn apart the family unit God intended, we realize how much of a building block it is for society. Though land and cattle in more modern dress have become large and small businesses, mutual funds and investment portfolios, such items are basic for our economy.

For many of us the problem is not that we don't have such things but that we have grown *accustomed* to having them in abundance. So many of us have eaten for so long from the smorgasbord table groaning under the weight of God's plenty, that we have forgotten that important word *need*. "All I *need* to keep my body and life," Luther said, not "all I *want*." Then when the heavenly provider removes a dish or two from that table, when he doesn't serve up for me the health and wealth, the money and goods, the house and business, the family circumstances I *want*, all I do is complain. Instead of looking around at what I need and looking up at him who provides it, I grumble as if I've been shortchanged by his still more than generous hand. Daily I need to see his hand behind it all. Daily I need to see his wisdom dispensing the portions according to my needs.

What he uses

My heavenly Father can do anything. That's what it means when I call him almighty. Of course, he could multiply the bread in my cupboard and the meat in my fridge, as he once did the barley loaves and small fishes for the five thousand. Certainly he could heal my diseases directly, as he once did for the lame and the blind. Miracles we call them, and they can still happen today.

Far more frequently, though, my Father provides for me through what we call natural means. He who once told Adam "By the sweat of your brow you will eat your food" (Genesis 3:19) expects me to get a job and gain my daily sustenance in that way. He who once healed King Hezekiah's fatal infection with a fig poultice (2 Kings 20:7) expects me to go to the physician and follow his advice. The overly enthusiastic who expect God's hand to open and provide without the callouses of effort on their own hands have no scriptural leg on which to stand. The overly apprehensive who fail to see God's hand behind their needed provisions are also heading for a fall. The old adage still stands: "Do your best and let God do the rest."

What he removes

"Richly and daily providing . . . all I need for body and life." Do I really believe those words, or do I sometimes weary myself with worry? My Father is not far off in the heavens—unawares, uncaring, and unavailable. He's right beside me with his hands wide open to provide for my needs. When changing circumstances blur my focus on his providing hand, then more than ever I need to see the nail-pierced hands of his dearly loved Son. How can a Father who "did not spare his own Son, but gave him up for us all—how will he not also, along with him, graciously give us all things?" (Romans 8:32).

Ants scurrying and hurrying around in consternation and concern? No! Rather, children casting all their anxiety on him, knowing because they have stood beneath his Son's cross, he cares for us!

Prayer: Father, show us daily how well you have provided for our souls, so that we trust you to provide richly and daily all that we need for our body and life. Amen.

The First Article

"God also preserves me by defending me against all danger, guarding and protecting me from all evil."

Flashing red lights and numerous security people—that's what we saw when we finally landed in Minneapolis. Because Air Force One was coming in, our flight had to circle for an extra half hour. Then with the president safely on the ground, we could land. Moreover, all those security people were there to guard and protect and keep him safe on the ground.

As God's children, we have even better security than the president of our country. We have a loving heavenly Father who keeps us safe by defending us against all danger and guarding and protecting us from all evil.

What can I expect?

What can I expect from my heavenly Father? Daniel, prophet of God, can you tell us? "There I was hurtling down toward those hungry lions. I could almost feel the swipe of their claws and the bite of their teeth, but nothing happened. I moved among those hungry lions in their den all night long and they never touched me. You know why? Because the true God of Israel whom I served sent an angel to stand beside me. My God defended me against this danger and guarded and protected me from this evil."

What can I expect from my heavenly Father? Peter, can you tell us? "There I was, arrested by villainous

King Herod, locked in chains in a maximum-security cell, sandwiched between two guards, expecting the worst. Herod had already killed my fellow apostle James. Imagine my surprise when an angel tapped me on the shoulder, struck off my chains, and told me to follow him right out the prison door. I could hardly believe it. The Christian friends at whose apartment door I knocked could hardly believe it either. But I told them who had done it. It was the Lord, whose saving name I preached, who defended me against this danger and guarded and protected me from this evil."

Now it's our turn to speak. Perhaps some of us can point to dramatic ways the Lord has rescued us. Was it safety under a surgeon's scalpel, only minor bumps and bruises in a freeway accident, missing an airline flight that later crashed? Each one of us can write in his own example, either for himself or his loved ones. In such events the protecting hand of our heavenly Father is very visible.

What about those more numerous times when his protection goes unnoticed? What about the morning after morning I rise refreshed from sleep without a clue about the danger he kept away from me that night? What about my coming and going day after day without a thought about the hurt he prevented and the evil he diverted? What would I see if, just for one day, the Lord would open my eyes and let me see the many times he defended me or my loved ones against danger and guarded and protected us from evil?

How can I be sure?

But doesn't experience teach us painfully that sometimes danger strikes and evil succeeds? Tell us, Joseph, about how it's no fun to lose your family and freedom as a teenager because of your brothers' envy. No fun to languish in a prison cell because of a spurned woman's lies. No fun to face a situation for which there seems to be no solution. But tell us also, Joseph, how years later—raised to the vice presidency of Egypt and reunited with your family—you saw how God used the evil your brothers thought against you to keep alive his people, his people from whom the Savior would come.

Again it's our turn to speak. Each one can write in his own experiences. In confirmation class we learned that "in all things God works for the good of those who love him" (Romans 8:28). Yet it's from experience, more than from memorization, that we learn the truth of that promise. Sometimes the good becomes apparent rather soon. Sometimes it takes years, as with Joseph in Egypt. Sometimes we'll have to wait until eternity's shores. Always the divine equation holds true: GOD + "EVIL" = GOOD.

I look around me and see no flashing red lights or security guards. I look up and see a loving, almighty Father. Those who dwell under the shadow of his wings are always safe.

Prayer: Thank you for the many times you daily protect and defend me. Help me look to you in times of trouble and days of distress, so that I trust your loving guidance. Amen.

The First Article

"... by defending me against all danger, guarding and protecting me from all evil ..."

Have you ever seen an angel? Me either. Nor do we need to. It's enough to know what David knew: that "the angel of the Lord encamps around those who fear him, and he delivers them" (Psalm 34:7). Sent by a heavenly Father to watch over his children, the angels help defend us against all danger and guard and protect us from all evil.

Our Father's messengers

There's much we don't know about the angels. Though Scripture speaks about them with frequency and familiarity, there's little detailed information about their creation, nature, and rank. Instead the inspired record centers on their activity. Even the name they are given—angels—centers on their activity. For that word means "messenger." So they are God's messengers sent to carry out the wishes of their Creator.

In heaven that activity involves standing round the throne of the holy triune God and singing his praises. So powerful is the angelic choir that heaven's doorposts and thresholds shake at the sound of their voices (Isaiah 6:4). In eternity it'll be our joy to join them as together we raise the powerful anthem giving all "praise and glory and wisdom and thanks and honor and power and strength to our God for ever and ever" (Revelation 7:12).

At the heart and center of their activity is their service to God's people. The author of Hebrews wrote of the angels, "Are not all angels ministering spirits sent to serve those who will inherit salvation?" (1:14). Who was sent to deliver hesitant Lot from the soon-to-be-destroyed, debauched city of Sodom? Who was dispatched to hold the mouths of the lions in the den into which brave Daniel had been hurled? Who was commissioned to instruct the aged, childless priest Zechariah? the divinely graced virgin Mary? the concerned husband-to-be Joseph? Who was charged to watch over the holy family during their flight into Egypt and then their return to Nazareth? From our Bible history days, we know the answer. God's angels, those invisible creatures he had made particularly to serve his children, were given those tasks.

His children's protectors

Remember what Satan did to Job with God's permission? He stripped him of his flocks, struck down his children, and shattered his health—though God reversed it all in the end. The old evil foe is still roaming the world, looking for the "Jobs" of today. He just cannot tolerate seeing believers taking God at his Word and walking his ways. Even more so, he "sees red" when believers carry God's saving Word out into the world. So he attacks again and again with all the "powers of this dark world" and all the "spiritual forces of evil" (Ephesians 6:12). Against such a formidable foe, who of us can stand? Facing him with our own muscle power is like fighting a fire with a squirt gun. Battling him one-on-one is like sending a kindergartner into the ring against the heavyweight champion of the world.

Is there no help against the spiritual and physical damage Satan would inflict on us? God's children know the answer. Again and again they have experienced the truth expressed by the psalmist: "If you make the Most High your dwelling—even the LORD, who is my refuge—then no harm will befall you, no disaster will come near your tent. For he will command his angels concerning you to guard you in all your ways; they will lift you up in their hands, so that you will not strike your foot against a stone" (Psalm 91:9-12). Through his messengers our Father bears us up on eagles' wings and holds us in the palm of his hand.

So we go about our daily life trusting that the angels are there, even though we cannot see them. And when the end of our earthly life draws near, we still look for those angels. They who once carried Lazarus' soul to Abraham's bosom in heaven will safely cradle my soul also. They who will come with the returning Savior to gather the elect for the final judgment will safely number me with the sheep on his right hand.

Never see an angel So what? Better to see that when the Bible speaks of them, it places the emphasis not on these invisible messengers but on the loving God who sends them and what he so graciously does through them.

Prayer: Heavenly Father, "let your holy angel be with me, that the wicked foe may have no power over me." Amen.

The First Article

"All this God does only because he is my good and merciful Father in heaven, and not because I have earned or deserved it."

"Hope he gets what he's got coming." Ever say or think those words? It's difficult not to. When someone has been unkind to us or hurt us in some way, the human reaction is retaliation or revenge. Somehow, someway we hope that person will receive his just deserts.

Is that how the Lord reacts to and deals with us? Are his providing for the needs of body and soul and his protecting, guarding, and defending of us our just deserts? Or is the answer something much more wonderful, something that we can find explained only in the heart of a loving heavenly Father?

What we've got coming

Quickly tell me just one thing we have done that God should do so much for us. Name me just one action that has so impressed God in heaven that he should feel obliged to do something in return. Can't think of any? Neither can I. All that I can think of, if I'm honest, is how much like the prodigal in Jesus' parable I am. I've despised and never fully appreciated my Father's love. I've abused his blessings and taken them for granted. I've broken his heart as I've helped crucify his Son on Calvary and wound him anew with my daily forgetfulness and failings. The best I deserve to hear from him is

27

the answer "That's right" to my confession: "I am no more worthy to be called your son."

The elderly father had a son who, over the years, had broken his heart again and again. When that son came crawling back after another incident, I told the father, "If that were my boy, I wouldn't take him in." "That's the difference," the father responded, "he's not your boy. He's mine, and I love him." That man's reaction was not based on his son's lovableness but on a father's love. How much more so with our Father in heaven. Human fathers, as they deal with their unlovable children, may, at times, faintly imitate the love of our heavenly Father. Never, though, can they duplicate the depth of love the heavenly Father showed when he sacrificed his precious Son for out-and-out sinners and outright enemies like us.

What we get instead

The best robe as a status symbol on his shoulders, the signet ring of authority on his finger, the sandals of a freeman on his feet, the fattened calf reserved for some special occasion roasting on the spit—full treatment as a son—that's what the undeserving prodigal in Jesus' parable received from a good and merciful father. Freezers filled with food and closets with clothes, more than a passable place to lay my head, loved ones standing at my side, angels watching over me, dangers deflected from my daily path, evil turning into good—all that and much more is what we undeserving prodigals receive from our good and merciful heavenly Father.

The translation of Luther's words learned in my catechism days still resonates in my head. "All this purely out of fatherly, divine goodness and mercy" were the words I memorized. Usually human goodness responds to what it has received, to what is required, or to what is offered as a reward. Divine goodness stands above all such selfish motives. It gives because it has to. It gives because that is its very nature. Not the nature of the recipient, but the nature of the giver dictates what is done.

"Mercy" is the quality that sees need and responds to it. Again, human mercy is so often predicated on what we might receive back from the one we've helped, on what others might think if we don't help, or on what God might give us in return. Divine mercy *is above all that.* It rises in a Father's heart that is truly unselfish. It reaches out to those who are truly undeserving. It takes care even of the enemy and, more so, of his children.

That's not just the Creator and Preserver of all who opens his hand and satisfies the desire of every living thing. That's *my Father,* whose goodness is divine and whose mercy is matchless. From him I receive not what I've got coming, but what his divine goodness and mercy give instead.

Prayer: I thank you, heavenly Father, for what your goodness and mercy do for me. Help me to appreciate that goodness and mercy. Help me to imitate it toward others. Amen.

The First Article

"For all this I ought to thank and praise, to serve and obey him.

This is most certainly true."

How come we're better at taking than thanking? And how come we seldom say thank you to those who do the most for us? Like our heavenly Father, for example. No, he doesn't need our thank yous. He keeps on doing what he does for us whether he receives our thanks or not. The need for thanksgiving lies not with him but with us. For us it is important to express our gratitude for all he does, and there's joy to be found in such thanksgiving.

From our heart

Gratitude is not some picture you put up on the wall or some statement that starts outwardly on the lips. Behind the joyous hymn text "Now thank we all our God with hearts and hands and voices" lies a grateful heart. Even the sweetest "Gloria in Excelsis" falls flat if the heart is not tuned right.

Heartfelt gratitude centers more on the giver than on the gift. As Paul, referring to the offering for the needy he was gathering, once told the Christians in Corinth, "What I want is not your possessions but you" (2 Corinthians 12:14), so a thankful believer tells his Father, "What I want is not your gifts but you." A faith that ties us to the heavenly Father for what he is and not merely for what he does is truly a divine gift and will be the most joyous. Such a faith thanks God in plenty and in want, in green pastures or in the valley of the shadow—when it feels God's goodness and when it doesn't. The sheer joy of knowing him as our Father prompts thanksgiving.

Thanksgiving then follows *for whatever* the Father sends. When the sun is shining and the rain falling, when work is successful and life sweet, when we're healthy and happy and have family and friends, we thank the giver. But we also thank him when life is not so smooth and the way not so easy. When suffering numbs our mind or pains our body, we trust his care and give thanks. When death claims a loved one or chases after us, we look for eternal gain and give thanks. When tears blot the pages of life's journal, we compose the most precious hymns of praise. Our Father wants, on his lap, a child in whose eyes the light of gratitude shines—regardless.

With our life

If only we could telegraph a floral bouquet or write a note to our heavenly Father, just to show how thankful we are. Though nobody delivers to heaven, and God doesn't have a mailbox, yet we have ways of expressing our gratitude to him. Luther lines them up for us. He says it is our duty to thank him. Like Noah, fresh off the ark after the flood, we can build our altars of thanksgiving to our Father for all he does and gives. Those prayers before and after meals, in the morning and in the evening, behind our steering wheels and at our desks need to start not with requests but thanksgiving.

"To praise him." Like the shepherds returning to their homes and flocks after kneeling at the manger bed of

God's greatest gift, we can glorify him. First we turn to him, as those shepherds did and as we can do in our worship services, and thank him for what he has given us. Then we go out to the streets of life, again like those shepherds, to spread the Word. Praise involves these two sentences: "Look what he has done for me. Look what he can do for you."

"To serve him." Like the woman who washed Jesus feet with her tears and precious perfume, we kneel before him. My dollars and cents are not really mine, but his—to be used to take care of my family, help the needy, support the government, and supply the means for my church and synod to spread the real treasure. My moments and my days are not really mine, but his—to be used in Christian love and concern toward all around me. My abilities and talents are not really mine, but his—to be used in my home, my community, and my church: *for him.*

"To obey him." Whether young, old, or in between, the grateful believer prays daily, "Make me to walk in your commands—'tis a delightful road—nor let my head or heart or hands offend against my God" (CW 462:4). Just as the test of creed is deed, so the test of gratitude is the life we lead.

Take my heavenly Father for granted? Luther was right: "For all this I ought to thank and praise, to serve and obey him. This is most certainly true."

Prayer: Heavenly Father, help me daily to be thankful to you for being my Father and for all that you do for me. Amen.

The Second Article of the Apostles' Creed

I believe in Jesus Christ, his only Son, our Lord, who was conceived by the Holy Spirit, born of the virgin Mary, suffered under Pontius Pilate, was crucified, died, and was buried. He descended into hell. The third day he rose again from the dead. He ascended into heaven and is seated at the right hand of God the Father almighty. From there he will come to judge the living and the dead.

What does this mean?

I believe that Jesus Christ, true God, begotten of the Father from eternity, and also true man, born of the virgin Mary, is my Lord.

He has redeemed me, a lost and condemned creature, purchased and won me from all sins, from death, and from the power of the devil, not with gold or silver but with his holy, precious blood and with his innocent suffering and death.

All this he did that I should be his own, and live under him in his kingdom, and serve him in everlasting righteousness, innocence, and blessedness, just as he has risen from death and lives and rules eternally.

This is most certainly true.

The Second Article

"I believe that Jesus Christ, true God, begotten of the Father from eternity . . ."

"To my dying day I'll never understand," said the clerk behind the car rental desk in that small midwestern airport. Waiting for my flight, I had struck up a conversation with him, and he was telling me his story. As a young soldier in World War II, he had hit Normandy Beach and had survived. Later his unit had been dispatched to the Pacific theater, but his name had been pulled. While seven out of ten of his buddies perished in an island assault, he was safe in the United States. How come? It was beyond his understanding, but not his belief, because there he stood behind that rental desk.

Far more beyond our understanding, and yet far more vital for our believing, is the grand truth Martin Luther puts before us as we begin our study of the Second Article.

Beyond our understanding

In the First Article we saw God, wonderful as a creator and careful as a provider—but a God more afar off. In this Second Article, we see God right in our midst, indeed, right in our flesh. The God of all creation comes not just to live among his creatures but as one of them. Even more, in God come into the flesh we see God revealed. To see Jesus is to see God. To behold Jesus' heart throbbing with love is to have a close-up of what the Father's heart is like. His is not just the heart of a creator and preserver but also that of a compassionate Father who yearns for the return of his fallen creatures and makes it possible by sending his only Son.

"Jesus" his Son is named, meaning "Jehovah saves." Many others carried that name, but none like him. "Christ" he is titled, meaning the "anointed one." Other prophets, priests, and kings were anointed in Old Testament times, but none ever served like him. And he is "Lord." Other kings come, not even rating a single line in the history books, but he reigns forever and ever.

All this because he is "Jesus Christ, his only Son," "true God, begotten of the Father from eternity." Don't expect me to explain what those terms all mean. They are beyond our understanding. We are God's sons, made by him and then remade by him through spiritual birth. Jesus Christ is God's Son not by birth or creation but as true God with the Father and the Spirit from eternity. "Begotten from eternity" is just using human terms to say what we can't explain. It's our way of declaring that Jesus Christ is "very God of very God," with all the qualities and attributes of God in all their fullness.

How can this be? How can the infinite Lord be confined in human skin? How can he who belongs to eternity also become part of history? To the human mind such a thought is preposterous and worthy only of rejection. But not for you and me. We know that Jesus Christ came as God incarnate to save lost mankind before he comes again to judge it.

Not beyond our believing

How do we know? Were we there that night the Christmas angels described the Bethlehem baby as

"Christ the Lord"? Were we there at the Jordan 30 years later when the Father from heaven said of the just-baptized Jesus, "This is my beloved Son"? Were we there that week after Easter when a turned around Thomas, kneeling before the risen Jesus, exclaimed, "My Lord and my God"? There's more. Not only does Jesus carry the names of God; he does what only God can do. Who but the almighty God could raise a dead lad being lugged to a cemetery on a funeral stretcher? Who but the all-knowing God could tell Nathanael before they ever met, "I saw you under the fig tree"? Who but the ever-present God could tell his disciples shortly before he left them for heaven, "I am with you always"? And who but the all-gracious God could tell the woman who was a sinner, "Go in peace, your sins are forgiven"?

No, we weren't there to see these things, but we believe them. God has told us about them in his Word, and his Word is true. Moreover, his Spirit has removed unbelief's dense cataracts from our eyes so that we see them just as surely as if we'd been there. That's part of what it means when we say "I believe in Jesus Christ, his only Son, our Lord." But he's not just a person about whom I know something or about whom I learned something in my catechism days. He's true God from all eternity, come to earth to take me to his heaven.

Beyond our understanding? Absolutely! Beyond our believing? No! Thank God and his grace for that!

Prayer: Dear Jesus, our God and Lord, thank you for coming to earth. Help us marvel daily at the love behind the mystery of your coming into our flesh to save us. Amen.

The Second Article

". . . and also true man, born of the virgin Mary . . ."

Really human? In over 30 years of teaching adults in
confirmation classes, I can hardly remember that question being asked. Often the question arose whether
Jesus was true God, but not whether he was true man.
Was this biblical truth something taken for granted by
people who were all too aware of what it meant to be
human? Or was the deep meaning behind this truth
missed, so that people merely nodded their heads in
agreement and then hurried on?

What are our thoughts as we hear Luther say of our Jesus
that he is "also true man, born of the virgin Mary"?

Like us in so many ways

Browse the pages of the Old Testament, and you find
our Savior's humanity stressed. "Seed of the woman,"
God described him, tracing his genealogy back to our
first ancestors, Adam and Eve. "A prophet like me from
among your own brothers," Moses detailed him, pointing Israel to the Savior coming not only *for* them but
also *from* them.

Enter the stable at Bethlehem that holy night, and you
see his humanity. A mother goes through labor pains, and
a child is born. The baby, warm from his mother's womb,
is sheltered in her arms and sustained at her breast. Stand
in the shadows, and watch as the baby grows into a child,
a teen, an adult. He has to learn and does learn as we do,

progressing from stage to stage of knowledge. His body, like ours, feels the need for daily food to sustain him and for nightly sleep to rejuvenate him.

Things that move our souls also moved his. In the wilderness, he was buffeted by the continued assaults of Satan. In the temple, he felt the flash of righteous anger at what was being done to his Father's house of prayer. At the grave of his friend Lazarus, he shed bitter tears over death's reign. In the garden, he sweat bloody drops under an inhumane load. On the cross, he knew the anguish of a pain-racked body. And in the grave, they buried his lifeless clay.

How could this be? How could the almighty Creator become a creature? How could he submit himself to our existence and subject himself to our experiences? We know the answer. With God all things are possible—and we trust his almighty power enough to believe that he could become a true man like us. Far more important for us is the question why? Why would God want to become our brother? Simply because we can't come to him. So he comes to us and in a most wonderful way. When we see the Lord of heaven and earth entering our world as a little baby, experiencing the same pains and problems as his creatures—even exhaling his final breath as we do in death—how can we doubt his love. This Jesus is true man come to earth in wondrous, divine love so that we might go to his heaven.

Unlike us in some vital ways

We, however, have some things Jesus did not. We are born with a sinful nature, inherited from sinful parents. Because of that natural corruptness, our thoughts, words, and deeds daily go awry. When God looks down on us from heaven, he sees only creatures who, like sheep, have gone astray and turned each one to his own way. When we look up at God, we see only a righteous judge before whom we must shiver and shake in anticipation of his punishment.

But when we look at Jesus come into our flesh, we see "one who is holy, blameless, pure, set apart from sinners" (Hebrews 7:26). The man Jesus is "holy"—with not the smallest speck of sin's pollution to be found in him. He is "blameless"—having nothing base or bad attached to him. He is "pure"—undefiled morally by any inner defect or outward deviation from his Father's will. And he is "set apart from sinners"—living among sinners, yet not joining them in their sins. Never did he have to regret a single thought, word, or deed. Never did he have to shed a tear of repentance. Never did he have to pray for forgiveness. In him we see what God intends our life to be—one great whole of perfect love to God and to our fellow man. And, most important of all, through his perfect life and innocent suffering and death, we can become what he is, pure and holy in his and our Father's sight!

In a Christmas sermon preached in 1533, Luther mentioned a unique worship custom of the church in the Middle Ages. During the recitation of the Nicene Creed, he related how the congregation would bow reverently at the words "and became fully human." Not a bad thought when we stop to consider what those seemingly humble words "and also true man, born of the virgin Mary" all contain.

Prayer: Dear Jesus, thank you for becoming my brother and, above all, for being my Savior so that your Father and his home can be mine forever. Amen.

The Second Article

"I believe that Jesus Christ, true God, begotten of the Father from eternity, and also true man, born of the virgin Mary, is my Lord."

Do you like a mystery? I must confess that I do. Whether it's a book or a movie, it's fun to match wits with the writer and try to solve the case. Sometimes you win; sometimes you lose. But there's always a solution.

Our last two devotions placed a mystery before us. The one before last presented Jesus Christ as true God, and the last one presented him as true man. Does this mean there are two Jesus Christs, one divine and one human? That's not what the Scriptures say. They reveal a Jesus Christ who is God from all eternity, but who became man in the womb of the virgin Mary and is now true God and true man in one inseparable person.

Solve this divine mystery? No way, at least not this side of heaven. But we do need to look at it for it contains truths necessary for our salvation.

A mystery

To the Colossians Paul wrote, "In Christ all the *fullness* of the *Deity* lives in *bodily form*" (2:9). To Timothy he put it this way: "There is *one God* and one mediator between God and men, *the man* Christ Jesus" (1 Timothy 2:5). These inspired words lay the mystery of the God-man simply and clearly before us. Also these words deter us from mistakes that other mortal minds have made. It won't work to describe Jesus Christ as half-God and half-man or to present him as some homogenized blend like chocolate milk. Jesus Christ is true God and true man in one inseparable person— with not one ounce of his Godhead or humanity lost in the process, but mysteriously united in him.

So intimately united are God and man in Jesus that each nature shares in the attributes or qualities of the other. Consequently, Isaiah could describe the *child to be born* of the virgin as the "Mighty God, Everlasting Father" (9:6), and Paul could describe the *blood* shed on the cross as *God's* "own blood" (Acts 20:28). Similarly, man is not almighty, but because God became man, the risen Christ could tell his disciples, "*All authority* in heaven and on earth has been *given* to me" (Matthew 28:18). Because of the union of God and man in Jesus, Scripture can describe God as being born, becoming hungry and even dying. And it can describe man as having all power, wisdom, and being present everywhere.

Solve the mystery of Jesus the God-man? Don't even try. That's far more impossible than a mosquito trying to become an elephant or a two-year-old seeking to master Einstein's theory of relativity. Rather, let's stand in awe at this mystery and then at the saving love of God behind it.

A necessity

Why did the Savior have to be both divine and human? Our catechism summarizes, "So that he could be under God's law and also keep it perfectly for me" (Luther's Catechism, page 156). God came to earth to do what man could not do, keep the law perfectly. As God, he gave the law and was above it. As man, he put himself under all the demands of his holy law. As the God-man, he kept the law perfectly so that one day in heaven we can present to our holy God, who has a right to demand it, a perfect keeping of his law. If we could actually hold such a product in our hands, it would contain the initials MJC—"made by Jesus Christ." That's what Paul tells us in these well known words: "God sent his Son, born of a woman, born under law, to redeem those under law" (Galatians 4:4,5).

Why did our Savior have to be both divine and human? Our catechism further summarizes, "So that he could die and also ransom me by his death" (Luther's Catechism, page 156). As man, he could shed his blood and die—but such blood would have no power to free anyone from sin's punishment. As God, his blood would have the worth to pay for all sins, from the first Adam to the last. That's what the apostle John tells us also in some well-known words: "The blood of Jesus, his Son, purifies us from all sin" (1 John 1:7).

Get lost in the mystery of how Jesus Christ could be both God and man? Scripture doesn't. Instead, and very simply, it tells us that God became a child for one purpose—to save us. And then, very simply, it reminds us that we also need to become children—for only with the God-given faith of a child can we accept the mystery and rejoice in the necessity of Jesus Christ, true God and true man, our Savior.

Prayer: Dear Lord Jesus, may I always worship you as the God-man, my Savior. Amen.

The Second Article

"He has redeemed me, a lost and condemned creature . . . not with gold or silver but with his holy, precious blood and with his innocent suffering and death."

It was almost humorous. Waiting for the bus at the airport, I watched as an illegally parked car was being towed away. Behind it ran the driver who had parked there, but the tow truck didn't slow down. The only way this unfortunate man could retrieve his car was to go to the pound and pay the fine.

I saw some humor in that scene, but there's none at all in the words Luther puts before us. Souls, lost in sin's bondage and condemned to hell's prison, are no laughing matter. Neither is there humor in the price Jesus Christ, the God-man, had to pay to redeem them, to set them free.

The need for our redemption

Lost is a terrible word. It sets before our minds the sight of a little child *separated* from its parents in the huge department store and sobbing inconsolably. Only the *lostness* of which Luther speaks is far more terrible. Mankind, whom God created to walk peacefully at his side in perfect fellowship with him, now does not see God's loving face turned toward him but his righteous back. A perfect home, where God is always present with all his favor, is now replaced with a world that is laced with sin and a future locked up in the cells of hell. And hearts, once filled with complete holiness and knowledge of their loving God, have shriveled into organs that are capable only of resisting and rebelling against him, their loving Creator.

Condemned is also a terrible word. It reminds us that the lost sinner—even if he would want to—can't repair his heart or rebuild the road back to God or buy himself loose from sin's bondage or build up again a proper relationship with God. All he can do is shiver under God's righteous anger over sin already on earth and shudder in anticipation of facing that anger in eternity. Sinful man may not always recognize or acknowledge his dismal condition, but that doesn't alter the fact that "all have sinned and fall short of the glory of God," and that "death came to all men, because all sinned" (Romans 3:23; 5:12). No, nothing humorous here; rather, man's desperate need for redemption.

The cost of our redemption

The cost for sinful mankind's redemption was obviously much higher than the cost paid by the driver to get his car back from the pound. In fact, all the silver and gold in the world wouldn't buy back just one soul. God himself set the price. And he loved us enough to pay it. "Without the shedding of blood there is no forgiveness," he had the sacred writer record (Hebrews 9:22). Again and again, he reminded his people Israel of this fact (as the blood of those animal sacrifices flowed). Blood was required— "holy" and "precious" blood. The Lamb to be slain was none other than his own sinless Son. And since it was divine blood, it was precious and powerful enough to cleanse from every guilty stain.

"Innocent suffering and death" was also part of the ransom Christ paid for sinners. We think we know something about suffering when we feel sickness' sharp pain, loss' salty tears, disappointment's stunning blow. But never in our wildest imagination does our suffering come close to his. The bruised flesh, beaten back, and bloodied scalp he endured as they hung him on that instrument of torture called a cross; the pains of hell and full punishment for every sin of every sinner—how do we even begin to assess what he suffered. And all this was heaped upon one who was himself completely innocent. Think what the media would make of the execution of this innocent Jesus today. Above all, think of what a just and loving God made out of it in his heaven. For here was the divine payment—written in the crimson ink of his Son's blood, covering the full cost needed to buy lost mankind back from the clutches of sin, death, and the devil. And most comforting of all, think of what we can make out of his innocent suffering and death. Let these words rush forth from our grateful hearts as they did from the apostle Paul: "[He] loved me and gave himself for me" (Galatians 2:20).

No, there is nothing humorous about the price God had to pay to redeem us. The proper word is joy— joy that is centered in God's redeeming love, joy that sustains us in every phase of life, and joy that is just itching to praise God face-to-face in heaven.

Prayer: "Grace and life eternal in that blood I find;
blest be his compassion, infinitely kind." Amen.
(CW 103:2)

The Second Article

"... purchased and won me from all sins, from death, and from the power of the devil ..."

It would have been nice to have had a big brother who could have played ball with me and taken me fishing. It would have been especially nice when I got into those inevitable scraps with other boys in the neighborhood. When they were bullying me around, I could have called my big brother—and he would have put them in their place.

Isn't that what Jesus has done for us? He went up against the biggest bullies we could ever face and punched them out. Though sin, death, and the devil still come back at us daily, they really can't hurt us if we call our big brother, the Redeemer, Jesus Christ.

Victory over sin

But doesn't sin still rule in this world? Aren't its grimy fingerprints clearly imprinted on the philosophy, lifestyle, and practices of those around us? Don't even the best of Christians still feel sin's shackles as they slip into thoughts, words, and deeds they do not want to? So what do you mean "Christ has purchased and *won* us from all sin"?

Time to look again at our big brother, Jesus. Onto the cross and into the fires of hell he took all that God could possibly demand of us because of our sin. "It is finished," he said of sin's payment—yours, mine, and the world's. So when Satan still comes, as he often does, to scoff about God not wanting us because of our sins, we need only point to Jesus' cross and repeat Paul's shout of victory: "There is now no condemnation for those who are in Christ Jesus" (Romans 8:1).

Moreover, Christ has freed us from sin's power. "Sin shall not be your master," Paul reminds us (Romans 6:14). When Satan cracks the whip, we need no longer jump as his slaves. With Christ's power we can turn up our noses at him and send him packing. When we don't—the fault lies not with our big brother but with us. We aren't using Christ's power as we might. And we need to stand closer in Christ's powerful shadow through Word and sacrament.

Victory over death

But doesn't death still rule in this world? Doesn't mankind shudder at the thought of it, seek to elude it, and finally succumb to it? If we're honest, we'd have to confess that death is not our favorite subject either. So what do you mean "Christ has purchased and won us from death"?

Time to look again at our big brother, Jesus. Paul reminds us that he "has destroyed death" (2 Timothy 1:10). Like children raiding the cookie jar and leaving not even a crumb, so Christ has wiped out death. When the Savior paid in full for sin, he also eliminated sin's wage, the bully known as death. As a result, when our soul must leave our body at journey's end, it's not bound for hell. It's bound for heaven. And death is but the elevator that whisks us there. When death still fogs our hearts with fear, then it's time to stand closer in Christ's shadow through Word and sacrament.

Victory over the power of the devil

Doesn't Satan stride across this world like some lion seeking whom he may devour? Doesn't he still, like some huge sumo wrestler, pin mankind to the mat? Doesn't he also overwhelm us at times with his massive strength? So just what do you mean "Christ has purchased and won us from the power of the devil"?

Time to look again at our big brother, Jesus. Satan can no longer accuse us, for that would be accusing our Redeemer. Satan can no longer control us, for that would be denying our Redeemer's victory. "The reason the Son of God appeared was to destroy the devil's work," John reminds us (1 John 3:8). If Satan still pins us at times as we "fight" our way through life, it's because we've drifted from the side of our big brother. Again it's time to stand closer in his shadow, using the victory he gives over the devil—until in heaven it is complete.

Jesus is our big brother? Certainly, but he is much more than that. He's our Redeemer who gives us the victory over sin, death, and the power of the devil.

Prayer: Dear Redeemer, we thank you for doing for us what no one else could do. Amen.

The Second Article

"... who was conceived by the Holy Spirit, born of the virgin Mary, suffered under Pontius Pilate ..."

Such humiliation! As I was following the hostess to the table in the crowded restaurant, I missed a step and pitched forward, flat on my face. Quickly I jumped up and brushed off her question of concern. But my ears were scarlet and my dignity was shredded.

That's not what Philippians 2:8 has in mind when it says that Christ Jesus " humbled himself and became obedient to death—even death on a cross!" When Scripture speaks of the Savior's state of humiliation, it refers to the God-man putting aside the full use of his heavenly power and glory. Though all the divine attributes were his, he generally chose not to use them. And for a most wondrous reason—that he might redeem us! During every worship service we speak of his humiliation and its saving purpose in the words of the Apostles' Creed.

Conceived by the Holy Spirit

Time to take our shoes off. With these words "conceived by the Holy Ghost," we step onto ground that is not just wonderfully holy but also divinely mysterious. In the Savior Jesus Christ, we see the mystery of God actually becoming man, of eternity being squeezed into time, and of him who fills all being confined in our history. There's no explanation for it—

but that doesn't make it any less true. The Jesus whom we confess in the Creed was not conceived by the ordinary process of nature but, as the Bible dares to state, by the miraculous working of the Holy Spirit.

Questions? Of course we have them. So did Mary when the angel announced her coming pregnancy. So did Joseph when he heard of that pregnancy. What's important is not to get lost in the mystery but to remember why it happened. If we do need a reminder, the words of the angel to Joseph will do: "What is conceived in her is from the Holy Spirit. She will give birth to a son, and you are to give him the name Jesus, because he will *save* his people from their sins" (Matthew 1:20,21). Did you catch the *why* in the angel's words? The Son of God humbled himself and was conceived by the Holy Spirit *to redeem us.*

Born of the virgin Mary

He who was and remains God from all eternity came into this world the same way we did—through the womb of a woman. Of no other of his creation did he become part, only of man. And he became human in every respect, as we are, except without the blight of sin. He took on our flesh and our sins, took them to Calvary's cross and into hell's inferno—and took them away forever. The sinless babe on the lap of a virgin mother was on his way to take our place on that Friday cross.

Listen carefully again as the inspired apostle puts into focus those words "born of the virgin Mary": God sent his Son, born of a woman, born under law, to *redeem* those under law, that we might receive the full rights of sons" (Galatians 4:4,5). Did you catch the *why* in Paul's words? The Son of God humbled himself and was born of the virgin Mary *to redeem us.*

Suffered under Pontius Pilate

More than any other in history, Pilate's name is remembered and repeated. We don't, however, envy him, because in the creed his name is linked with the blood of God's own Son. There's the blood seeping through the cloak which was thrown over Christ's whip-torn back. There's the blood trickling down Christ's face from his thorn-crowned brow. There's the blood Pilate couldn't wash from his hands. Is there any wonder why his name remains an odious memory?

Can any of us say Pilate's name without also saying our own? Isn't the guilt of Jesus' blood also on our hands? Wasn't it for crimes that we had done that Christ groaned upon the tree? Thank God his innocent blood has paid for what our hands and feet, ears and eyes, mind and life have committed. Thank God Peter's words apply also to us: "You were *redeemed* . . . with the precious blood of Christ, a lamb without blemish or defect" (1 Peter 1:18,19). Again did you catch the *why* in Peter's words? The Son of God humbled himself and suffered under Pontius Pilate *to redeem us.*

No longer need we stand before the holy God with our consciences burning and our hope for an eternal future with him shredded. God himself came to earth and put aside the use of his power and glory *to redeem us!*

Prayer: "Alleluia! Sing to Jesus . . . [he] redeemed us with his blood." Amen. (CW 169:1).

The Second Article

"... was crucified, died, and was buried ..."

How far down could he go? We were standing in the town square in St. Johns, Antigua, West Indies, watching a slender, smoothly jointed fellow doing the limbo. Down and down he lowered the crossbar until it was about a foot off the ground. And still he made it under.

Our Redeemer lowered himself much farther. How far down he went is not measured in inches or feet but in the words "was crucified, died, and was buried."

Was crucified

How far down did our Redeemer go? "He humbled himself and became obedient to death—even death on a cross," Paul reminds us (Philippians 2:8). Jesus not only died, but he died the most horrible death known in his day—perhaps in any day. Crucifixion was designed to make the victim suffer as much and as long as possible. So horrible was the cross that no Roman citizen was ever to hang on one. It was reserved for the worst of miscreants, the worthless alien—and God's holy Son.

Why didn't the God-man, with just a flick of his little finger, pluck those penetrating nails from his limbs? Why didn't he, with just a little glance of his mighty eyes, level those blasphemers parading beneath his cross with the ground? Why did he suffer the god-awful pain of the cross and the even greater godforsaken pain of hell? Listen to the apostle Paul again, "Christ *redeemed* us from the curse of the law by becoming a curse for us, for it is written: 'Cursed is everyone who is hung on a tree'" (Galatians 3:13). The Son of God humbled himself and *was crucified to redeem us.*

Died

Man is born to die. Though 21st-century man lives somewhat longer than his grandparents, yet the statistic ultimately remains the same: "One out of one dies." Death still waits patiently to clasp each of us in his cold arms. That was not what God had intended for man. But sin ruined it all, and ever since, the wages of sin has been death.

So why did Jesus have to die? There was nothing in him that deserved death. "The soul who sins is the one who will die," declares a holy God (Ezekiel 18:4). Yet he who had no sin died. In tremendous love our Savior collected the wage that a world of sinners had earned. In love beyond human comprehension, he felt the punishing anger of an offended God, the forsakeness of hell, the physical and mental pains of the damned. And with his death, he accomplished our redemption. "It is finished," he could cry, even as he laid his soul into the hands of his heavenly Father.

Days before it happened, he told his disciples, "The Son of Man did not come to be served, but to serve, and to give his life as a *ransom* for many" (Mark 10:45). At the time the disciples didn't understand his words, but after Calvary they did. So do we! He *died to redeem us.*

And was buried

Can you name a more desolate spot than a cemetery or a more heartrending scene than a burial? That's where we find the Redeemer in the last and lowest step of his humiliation. Courageous followers embalm and envelop his lifeless clay for deposit in a cold grave. Eyes that had surveyed a world of sorrow and shed tears of sympathy were now shuttered in death. Lips that had spoken so much healing wisdom were now silent and stripped of color. Hands that had helped the needy were now in need of a final burial act of love from friends. He who had life in himself was laid lifeless in a grave.

But don't forget how it goes on! "The third day he rose again." His empty grave in Joseph's garden turns everything into the Garden of Eden again. Job had it right: "I know that my *Redeemer* lives. . . . And after my skin has been destroyed, yet in my flesh I will see God" (19:25,26). *He was buried to redeem* us. And he has. Just wait until our graves open on the Last Day and our glorified bodies rejoin our souls and shout: "Alleluia, sing to Jesus. He *redeemed* us with his blood."

Prayer: "Hymns of praise then let us sing,
Unto Christ our heav'nly King,
Who endured the cross and grave,
Sinners to redeem and save, Alleluia." Amen.
(CW 157:2)

The Second Article

_____

"He descended into hell. The third day he rose again"

Everything was set. The team was returning with its second Rose Bowl victory in a row. As the first player came through the doors of the jetway, the crowd erupted into cheers. Through the streets and then in the stadium, the cheering continued. Our team had won.

How much more so on Easter Sunday. The Savior, who had humbled himself—putting aside the use of his power and glory—had won. The rescue mission that we know as redemption and that had brought Jesus down from his heavenly throne had been successful. And the Father who had sent his Son on that mission showed it by "[exalting] him to his own right hand as Prince and Savior" (Acts 5:31). So the next words of the Apostles' Creed remind us as they portray the victorious Redeemer fully and forever using his power.

He descended into hell

How quickly the cheering must have stopped and the mood shifted when the victorious Lord Jesus walked through hell's doors that first Easter Sunday. Imagine, if you can, the wild celebrating in hell when Jesus breathed his last on the cross. Satan seemed to have won the age-old battle for the souls of men. God had sent his champion, and there on the cross he hung, life-less and useless—or so it seemed. But when that champion, after having been made alive in the grave as the

55

first step of his exaltation, swept triumphantly through hell's gates, the demons of darkness scattered before him. In Colossians 2:15, Paul described the scene: "Having disarmed the powers and authorities, he [Jesus] made a public spectacle of them, triumphing over them by the cross." If hell had windows, the evil angels would have jumped out when the Redeemer came to proclaim his victory.

How come we so often act as if the devil were still celebrating? How come we so often live as if it were still Good Friday and Easter had never come? We can't blame the devil for getting up off the canvas after Easter's knockout blow. We should expect the master chameleon, as he sweats to hold the world captive in chaos and uncertainty, to camouflage defeat as victory.

But we know better. We have seen the Redeemer's victory parade into hell. So let the cheering continue! Let it even increase. Our sins are paid for. Satan has been defeated. Hell's doors have been padlocked. Heaven's doors are propped open. God has exalted Jesus as Prince and Savior.

The third day he rose again

Name the devil's greatest strength. It's death, isn't it? As the wage of sin, death puts us into Satan's grip and guarantees each sinner a cell number in hell's prison. Now name someone stronger than death. That has to be Jesus, doesn't it? The third day he rose victorious from the grave. Death couldn't hold him. He was God's Son—as he had professed to be. Sin's payment was finished—as he had proclaimed from the cross. Those who believed in him would never die—as he had promised. No wonder the early church lived so confidently and constantly in the light of that third day. To see how they did it, read through the book of Acts and note the numerous references to the Redeemer's resurrection. You might even highlight them so that, as you flip through the pages later, Christ's resurrection victory will jump out at you.

How come we so often act as if our Redeemer were still lifeless in the grave? How come we so often live as if it were still Saturday and Jesus' friends were rolling the stone ahead of his *filled* sepulcher? We should expect Satan to portray death as the grim reaper, sharpening his punishing scythe for us. We should not wonder when the old evil foe still tries to scare us with the threat of death as handcuffs that bind us for his hell.

But we know better! We have seen the Redeemer's emptied grave and his living presence. So let the cheering continue and even increase. The " third day" on which he rose is the greatest victory day the world will ever see. "He is risen" is the greatest victory shout the world will ever hear.

Prayer: Praise be to the God and Father of our Lord Jesus Christ! In his great mercy he has given us new birth into a living hope through the resurrection of Jesus Christ from the dead. Amen.

The Second Article

"He ascended into heaven and is seated at the right hand of God the Father almighty."

Don't you dislike "name droppers," people who try to impress you by claiming they have a connection with "big" names? People do pay attention to names. Some they admire. Others they despise. Some make it into the history books. Others only to the gravestone. But for many people, names are important.

In Philippians chapter 2, Paul tells of a name "that is above every name," a name at which "every knee should bow," a name that "every tongue [should] confess . . . is Lord." What might that name be? Christians don't need to ask. It's "Jesus," the only "name under heaven given to men by which we must be saved" (Acts 4:12). The exalted Redeemer's ascension into heaven and sitting at the right hand of God the Father almighty declare that Jesus has earned this name.

A coronation scene

What a glorious, not-to-be-forgotten scene that day out on the Mount of Olives. Once again, as they frequently had done during the 40 days since the resurrection, the disciples were standing with their beloved Redeemer. From his lips came words of assurance and promises of power. And then, while they watched, he stretched out his hands in blessing over them and slowly ascended into the sky until the hovering clouds covered him.

That was not only their God but their brother who was ascending—wearing the glorified form of their human nature. That was their brother who would continue to be their contact with a holy God. That was their brother whose precious face they would see again in eternity.

Far more glorious was what those disciples could not see. Their sinful human eyes could not gaze into heaven and behold the coronation scene Jesus' ascension actually was. The gates were opened wide, the flags flying at the top of their masts. The bands were playing and the banners waving—if heaven has such things. The trumpets were sounding and the angels singing. Before the throne stood God the Father with arms outstretched to welcome back his obedient Son. With his mission of redemption accomplished, the eternal Son now is draped with the full glory and displays the full power he had before his incarnation.

A comfort source

Christ's coronation was not retirement. His sitting at the Father's right hand did not involve his being placed, like some plaster statue, into some hall of fame. When Scripture speaks this way of the ascended Savior, it doesn't refer to location but to condition. Let the Scriptures themselves tell us what it means. In Ephesians 1:20-22 we read of the ascended Christ that "[God] seated him at his right hand in the heavenly realms, far above all rule and authority, power and dominion. . . . And God placed all things under his feet and appointed him to be head over everything for the church." If you think that means that Christ has the same divine power as the Father and that Christ rules over everything in heaven, earth, and hell and that

Christ always rules with the best interests of his believers in mind, you have a pretty fair idea of what his sitting at the Father's right hand includes. You also will know that these are not merely some ancient truths with no application for today but truths filled with sweet comfort for Christ's people of any day.

What comfort? When we as believers look at history, we don't see a world that seemingly is going nowhere—sputtering on and on until it runs out of steam. No. Instead, we look up at our ascended Lord and with eyes of faith see his strong hand guiding every detail of history and leading his people to victory and to the promised land.

What comfort? When we feel all alone in this world of fears and vale of tears, when hopes deceive and helpers fail, we look up at our ascended Lord. He's out of our sight—but we're not out of his. His loving and almighty hand is still stretched out over us as he guides us step-by-step toward his eternal glory.

What comfort? When the law curses us and Satan accuses us and our consciences condemn us, we look up at our ascended Lord. He's constantly pleading for us in heaven, stretching his nail-pierced hands toward the heavenly Judge to remind him and us that redemption is complete.

"Name dropping" can be distasteful, but not when it's Jesus' name. That name above all other names belongs on our lips constantly.

Prayer: "O Jesus, Shepherd, Guardian, Friend,
My Prophet, Priest, and King,
My Lord, my Life, my Way, my End,
Accept the praise I bring." Amen. (CW 358:5)

The Second Article

"From there he will come to judge the living and the dead."

Several years ago our state's public TV station aired a special about the eruption of Mount Vesuvius. The explosion of that volcano in 79 B.C. wiped out the cities of Pompeii and Herculaneum. The shoppers at the market, the rich in their baths, the slaves at their work were all dropped in their tracks by the superheated gasses and volcanic ash. The saddest part of the whole story was that not one of those people needed to die. Weeks of rumblings and shakings had preceded the actual explosion. But nobody paid any attention.

Scripture tells us plainly that the final act of our exalted Lord Jesus will be his return to judge the living and the dead. Again and again the New Testament speaks of this fact, even devoting one out of approximately every 25 verses in some way to his return and the judgment connected with it. The fact that it has not yet occurred is no reason to doubt its happening, but rather an indication of a gracious God granting ample time for the world to be ready for it.

Our Redeemer will do the judging

The world does its best to wish away Christ's return on the Last Day. Could this be because it doesn't know the judge as we do? He who returns to judge will be the same one who came the first time to save—the same one who was born of the virgin, bore the marks of the nails in his limbs, and was bruised on the accursed tree. Only his second coming will be far different than his first. When he returns, he will be splendid in all his glory—not shrouded in humility. He will be wielding all his divine power—not yielding it in human weakness. He will come to command— not to beseech. And all will have to obey him— whether they want to or not.

Does the thought of his return scare us? Not if we remember that the judge is our Redeemer. He's equipped us for the divine judgment by weaving our robe of righteousness with his perfect life and innocent death. He's dressed us for heaven by wrapping that robe around us in our baptism, and by daily draping it around us through his Word. What does it matter if we know not the time of his return—whether we're speaking about the last day of the world or our last day in it? By his grace we know how to be ready. Like the elderly widow who looked out her bedroom window each night and asked expectantly, "Tonight, Lord, tonight?" and each morning looked out that same window and asked, "Today, Lord, today?" so we look forward to the return of the judge who is none other than our Redeemer.

His judgment will be our final redemption

Our first glimpse of the Jesus we have never seen will be when he returns to judge the living and the dead. While we wait to see his lovely face, we use the time he gives to prepare ourselves for that day. Let others waste their time of grace, ignoring the cancer of sin that keeps eating away inside them. Let others expend foolish efforts in trying to predict the time of his return. When the last nation has heard his saving name and the last name has been written in his book of life, he will come. He has said so, and he does not lie.

When he does come, all will stand before his judgment throne. None will escape—from the billions still breathing on the earth's surface to those long blended back into the earth's dust. Nor will his judgment be arbitrary or capricious. "Whoever believes and is baptized will be saved, but whoever does not believe will be condemned," he has plainly stated (Mark 16:16). Our eternal future is directly tied to our relationship with the judge himself. So in a very real sense our judgment is being written right now—and on the Last Day, the heavenly judge will announce to the world what the verdict is.

What might we learn from the sure promise of his return to judge the living and the dead? What better lesson than, unlike the people of Herculaneum and Pompeii, to be watchful, preparing ourselves through use of Word and sacrament for his return. What better lesson than in our hours of sorrow and suffering here to look forward to his return when he, our Redeemer, will usher us into the complete redemption we know as heaven.

Prayer: Lord Jesus, keep our eyes on your Word so that we raise those eyes for your return. Amen.

The Second Article

"All this he did that I should be his own, and live under him in his kingdom, and serve him in everlasting righteousness, innocence, and blessedness, just as he has risen from death and lives and rules eternally.
This is most certainly true."

"STS," she answered. When I asked the college student sitting in my study why she was determined to take the hard road and do the right thing with the situation before her, she responded, "Don't you remember the motto for the Christian's life you gave us in confirmation class? It was STS—Saved To Serve."

She was right, as Luther reminds us in the closing words of his explanation for the Second Article. Previously he had held the spotlight on the Savior and all that he had done to redeem us. Now he reverses the spotlight and shines it on us, the redeemed, and what our response should be.

A new owner

A dog knows to whom it belongs—the owner who fills its dish, brushes its coat, and takes it for a walk. As a result, it's the owner whose voice that dog obeys, whose legs it wraps around, whose safety it protects. How much more so with the redeemed and their Redeemer. When Luther writes "All this he did that I should be his own, and live under him in his kingdom," he's issuing not a summons of what we should be but a statement of what we actually are. The apostle Paul well understood this. To Titus he wrote, "[Christ] gave himself for us to redeem us from all wickedness and to purify for himself a people that are his very own, eager to do what is good" (2:14). "Under new ownership" is the sign the believer carries with him in every aspect of daily life. He no longer is a doomed slave of Satan but a grateful-hearted, wholehearted servant of the one who has paid for him with his own blood.

Sounds good on paper, doesn't it? But is that the way it goes in our daily lives? Or does Satan bang on the door, more times than not successfully declaring that we still belong to him and demand that we still listen to him? In heaven "under new ownership" will be complete as we stand with perfect hearts and give perfect service to the Redeemer. Meanwhile, however, we need to sit beneath the cross of the Redeemer ever more frequently so that the price he paid for us provides the power we need to surrender our lives to him.

A new life

Luther sums up the new life of the redeemed with one word: *serve.* To that word he connects a number of thoughts, each one linked with the word *everlasting.* It's a service of "righteousness." Those who stand before God covered with Christ's robe of righteousness are also concerned about doing what's right in God's eyes. While their best efforts are still stunted and stained by sin, they trust Christ's righteousness to make them pleasing to their Lord.

It's a service of "innocence." Ever since the fall into sin, evil has ruled the human heart. Christ takes the believer back to paradise, back to that innocent state that allows us, at least in part, to walk with God and after God's ways. The Redeemer also points us heavenward to the time coming when we will no longer know, think, speak, or do any evil.

It's also a service of "blessedness." It's not what's *around* them but *inside* them that makes the redeemed truly happy. Blessedness involves knowing to whom we belong, knowing why we want to serve him, and then going at it in grateful love. Try as we might, there will always be something lacking in our service, but that doesn't rob us of our joy. It only drives us closer to our Redeemer, as we seek strength for renewed service to him, and draws our eyes heavenward where we will serve him perfectly night and day.

STS—saved to serve. That's what Luther so beautifully tells us as redeemed, restored, forgiven children of God. One last time he reminds us why and how with words that ring like some doxology: "All this . . . [because] he has risen from death and lives and rules eternally." Let our "Amen" also be "This is most certainly true."

Prayer: Risen Savior, help us to serve you faithfully each day until we serve you perfectly in heaven. Amen.

The Third Article of the Apostles' Creed

I believe in the Holy Spirit; the holy Christian church, the communion of saints; the forgiveness of sins; the resurrection of the body; and the life everlasting. Amen.

What does this mean?

I believe that I cannot by my own thinking or choosing believe in Jesus Christ, my Lord, or come to him.

But the Holy Spirit has called me by the gospel, enlightened me with his gifts, sanctified and kept me in the true faith. In the same way he calls, gathers, enlightens, and sanctifies the whole Christian church on earth, and keeps it with Jesus Christ in the one true faith.

In this Christian church he daily and fully forgives all sins to me and all believers.

On the Last Day he will raise me and all the dead and give eternal life to me and all believers in Christ.

This is most certainly true.

The Third Article

"I believe in the Holy Spirit..."

"The Holy who?" asked the man in my instruction class. Spirits were something out of science fiction, and ghosts were material for TV cartoons. To talk to him about a spirit, and a holy one at that, would take some doing. But he learned and appreciated it as the Holy Spirit worked in his heart through the Word. Later he became not only a member of the congregation but of the church council as well.

As we enter the Third Article of the Apostles' Creed and examine Luther's masterful explanation of that article, let's look at the Holy Spirit, in whom we say we believe.

Who he is

Don't be fooled. The word *spirit* does not imply that he is not real. He's not some faceless force flitting around out there, some impersonal energy that emerges and evaporates now and then. Though we cannot see him with the eye, we can feel him with the heart. That's one reason why his name comes from the Greek word *pneuma*, meaning "air." We who use pneumatic tires and pneumatic drills understand that—though we cannot see the air that fills the tire and drives the drill, it's very real.

The Holy Spirit is a "he," the third person in the triune God, true God with the Father and the Son, of equal power and majesty with them. As a real person, he teaches the Word of Truth, glorifies the Savior who stands at the center of truth, and convicts sinners so that they realize their need for saving truth. As a real person, he can be lied to—as Ananias and his wife, Sapphira, the first hypocrites in the New Testament church, discovered to their dismay (Acts 5:3,4). As a real person, he can be grieved by sinful responses to his work—as Paul warned the Ephesians not to do (4:30). To those who don't know God, he remains forever a mystery, "the Holy who?" But to those who confess "I believe in the Holy Spirit," he is a necessity, a divine person just as great and glorious as the Father and the Son.

What he does

His work is just as great and glorious as that of the Father and the Son. In fact, without his work all the efforts of the Father and the Son for our salvation would have been in vain. In eternity, God the Father planned the redemption of a world he had not yet made. In time, God the Son came into that ruined world and gave his blood as the ransom for its sin. But without the work of the Spirit, none would ever benefit. Salvation would be like some prescription gathering dust on the druggist's shelf, with no one ever knowing about it or wanting to use it.

Theologians call the necessary work of the Spirit *sanctification*. We might spell it "SAINTification," for that's what it really is. The work of the Spirit is to make saints out of us. No, we aren't talking about his turning us into super-Christians who have days named after us in the church year. We're talking about real saints, people whom the Holy Spirit has made holy by bringing them to the fountain filled with Jesus' blood and plunging them beneath that flood. The vital work of God the Holy Spirit is to create faith in the sinner's heart, so that the redemption planned by God the Father and prepared by God the Son becomes his very own. Without the Spirit's work, no one could stand as "saintified" before God or seek to serve him in his kingdom.

Do we sense the divine love behind our sainthood? God didn't merely create salvation by putting it into the world and then leaving it to the blind working of fate for us to find it. He didn't drop it down from heaven and then hope for our bumbling efforts to unearth it. He knew there was only one way. In saving love he takes the final step toward us and sends his Holy Spirit to sanctify us.

Our confession "I believe in the Holy Spirit" is tribute to divine love and grace!

Prayer: Lord, thank you for sending your Spirit to work faith in our hearts so that we are numbered among your saints on earth and in heaven. Amen.

The Third Article

"I believe that I cannot by my own thinking or choosing believe in Jesus Christ, my Lord, or come to him. But the Holy Spirit has called me by the gospel . . ."

Living, walking miracles. That's what you and I are. Around us are all kinds of *dead* people. Contrary to the old saying, dead people do talk. They talk and walk, live and work, eat and sleep, marry and have children. But they aren't *truly alive*. You and I are. As believers we are living, walking miracles of God. How so? Well, let's go into Luther's words and see.

We can't and won't

God made the human mind capable of so many things. With his intellect man designs skyscrapers and devises spaceships, unravels the genetic system, and unleashes nuclear power. Is there no limit to how far his mind can go? There is one "cannot" that besmirches it all. Ever since the fall into sin, man *cannot* believe in Jesus Christ as his Lord or come to him. God's plan of salvation is something entirely unknown to his thinking. Just look at the multitudes across the world who know nothing about Jesus Christ and him crucified. Even when man hears of God's plan of salvation, it remains something that is unacceptable to him. The gospel truths are "foolishness" to him, something "he cannot understand" because he doesn't have the spiritual mind required (1 Corinthians 2:14). In plain English, man, as he comes from his mother's womb, can't know or accept Jesus as his only Savior.

Not only can't he—he won't. "Not by my own choosing, " Luther further states. Even if man's thinking pointed to Christ, he wouldn't be able to choose him. "You were dead in your transgressions and sins" is the way Paul described former unbelievers (Ephesians 2:1). Even as a dead man can't jump-start his own heart so natural man can't jolt himself to faith. When confronted by the message of salvation, the unbeliever makes all sorts of moves—but not a single one of them toward Christ. Again, in plain English, the best he can do is continue to reject the Savior.

We so often take our faith in Jesus for granted! When's the last time you stopped to marvel at what the Holy Spirit has done for you? When's the last time you said, "I believe in Jesus Christ, my Lord," and then thanked the Spirit for the living, walking miracle he has made out of you, a former "can't and won't" unbeliever from your mother's womb.

He can and does

From beginning to end, Christian faith is the work of the Spirit. "No one can say, 'Jesus is Lord,' except by the Holy Spirit," Paul reminds us (1 Corinthians 12:3). Faith is something that must come from the outside, not the inside. Divine muscles are needed to smash the concrete-hard human heart if the seed of faith is to be planted there. Divine might is needed to pry open the paralyzed human hand if the treasures of Christ are to be held there. Again, in plain English, the Holy Spirit is the only one who can and does make believers out of us.

How does he work this miracle of faith? Did the crowd on Pentecost become believers because Peter preached or because of what he preached? Did the Eunuch of

Ethiopia trust in Christ because Philip hitchhiked a ride in his chariot or because of what Philip taught him while riding along the miles? Did young Timothy become wise unto salvation because his mother and grandmother trained him or because of what they told him? "He has called me by the gospel," Luther summarizes. The Holy Spirit works through the gospel, the good news of salvation, as we have it in Word and sacrament. "It [the gospel] is the power of God for the salvation of everyone who believes," Romans 1:16 reminds us.

This truth is also for our benefit. When faith loses spiritual wattage, we know where to turn for recharging. When we want loved ones to have Christ's treasures, we know what to tell them. When we send missionaries across our land and world, we know what they should carry to lost souls. It's the gospel! That's the power the Holy Spirit uses to bring people to their only Savior.

Living, walking miracles. That's what we are. And there are more like us because of the Holy Spirit who can and does work faith in the human heart through the powerful gospel.

Prayer: Thank you, Holy Spirit, for working in our hearts through the gospel of salvation. Help us bring it to others. In Jesus' name. Amen.

The Third Article

"... enlightened me with his gifts ..."

Ever been in a spot where there wasn't even the slightest speck of light? We were standing on a concrete platform deep in a cave. It was fenced all around with wire mesh. The park ranger warned us and then turned all the lights off. No one moved a muscle. You couldn't see a thing—not even the hand before your face. So dense was the darkness.

Made me think of the human heart that by birth has not even the slightest light of faith. Made me think also of the utter darkness of hell into which that heart is heading. Such would still be the condition of our hearts and the direction of our lives had it not been for the Holy Spirit enlightening us with the gifts God has for us in Christ.

He turns the light on

If only we could have been there on the first day of creation when light blazed out on a world that to that point had been shrouded in pitch darkness. The light did not arise from the darkness but was sent into it that life might exist in the world. All it took was one word—one creating word from God. What a glorious sight that must have been.

No less miraculous is what the almighty Lord works in our hearts. Hearts, pitch dark with unbelief and not even knowing it, need light. Hearts, having no capability to produce faith or even to desire it, need power from the outside. And that's what the Holy Spirit does for us. In 2 Corinthians 4:6, Paul marvels both at this miracle and the grace behind it as he writes, "God, who said, 'Let light shine out of darkness,' made his light shine in our hearts to give us the light of the knowledge of the glory of God in the face of Christ."

Most of us can't even remember when the Holy Spirit lit up our hearts with faith in the Savior. Nor is the moment all that important. Those wanting to pinpoint the moment usually are more concerned about pointing the finger of praise at themselves and *how they came* to faith. You and I want the finger of praise pointed where it belongs, at the Holy Spirit who *brought* us to faith, or to use Luther's words, who "enlightened me with his gifts."

Also, you and I know what the Spirit uses to create and to continue the light in our hearts. It's the gospel, the good news of salvation coupled with the water at the baptismal font, conveyed through the spoken and written Word, and connected with the elements in the Holy Supper. For us there's no aimless searching in the dark for some light switch, no looking for some circuit breaker to throw—but rather staying close to the Word and sacraments through which the Spirit transmits his electricity.

He turns the light up

The more the Spirit lights up our hearts in faith, the clearer the treasures we have by faith in Christ appear. What treasures you ask? More than the pile of gifts under even the best stocked Christmas tree. See that large one over there, wrapped in striking red ribbon? That's the best gift that a gracious God can give in

Christ—the forgiveness of sins we so desperately need and so joyously clutch to our hearts. Ask the penitent, crushed by his sin or the dying, looking back over his sin, what it means to have the Spirit shine the spotlight on this gift.

What's that compact one tied tightly to forgiveness? That's one that gets bandied about so much and yet is so little found—peace. No, not the more trivial kind among men and nations, but the much needed peace with a holy God—the peace that is ours through faith in Christ Jesus. Oh Spirit, don't ever take the spotlight off that gift.

Want to open some more gifts? What about that elusive one called hope? Not groundless hope that is just senseless dreaming but sure hope for heaven—hope anchored on Christ, the solid rock. Or what about confidence? Not whistling-through-the-cemetery-fooling-ourselves confidence, but the assurance that when God, who sent us Jesus, leads, the direction will always be right, regardless. Please, Spirit, turn up the light on these gifts; we need them so much.

And, Holy Spirit, please keep us ever mindful of how you turn up the light of faith in our hearts. Let the gospel be near and dear to us all our days.

Prayer: "Holy Spirit, Light divine,
Shine upon this heart of mine;
Chase the gloom of night away;
Turn the darkness into day." Amen. (CW 183:1)

The Third Article

"...sanctified..."

My wife wanted a miniature rose bush for her border. So we brought one home from the garden center, replaced the clammy, clutching clay with peat moss and vermiculite, and set the tiny bush into the new ground. Then we kept a close eye on that growing rose bush, just waiting for the first blossoms to appear. We did one more thing: we watered and fertilized that bush regularly.

The heavenly gardener whom we know as the Holy Spirit works much the same way with our hearts. He prepares the soil, plants faith, and then looks for blossoms. Along the way he also uses and expects us to use the fertilizer of the gospel.

Faith

"Without faith it is impossible to please God," the author of Hebrews declares (11:6). In gardening we accept this truth without reservation. If you want roses, you plant a rose bush. If you put a thistle plant into the ground, don't look for rose buds. If you think you can disguise that thistle plant by duct taping a handful of roses to it, the best you can expect is for those roses to shrivel. To have roses you need rose bushes.

Get the comparison? When God looks for lives that are sweetly scented to him, he looks first at the hearts behind those lives. Two worshipers may lay offering envelopes with identical amounts in the Sunday plate, but only the one brought by a heart expressing appreciation for the riches it has been given in Christ pleases God. Two neighbors may help the needy family next door, but only the deed coming from a heart reflecting the Savior's love brings a smile to God's face. When God looks for roses, he looks first, as we do, for a rose bush.

Here's where the heavenly gardener enters in. When Luther in this part of the Third Article speaks of the Holy Spirit sanctifying us, he's referring to the divine work involved in having people live Christian lives pleasing to God. As the very first step in the process, the Spirit must use the gospel's shovel to dig out the suffocating clay of unbelief and then plant faith's small rose bush in our hearts.

Fruit

"I am the vine; you are the branches. If a man remains in me and I in him, he will bear much fruit" Jesus declares (John 15:5). Again in gardening, here's a truth we accept without reservation. Rose bushes produce with increasing frequency as they mature. It's their very nature to flower, and we expect them to. If they don't, it won't be long before they're gone from the flower bed.

Again, get the comparison? When the heavenly gardener plants faith in our hearts, he expects that faith to blossom. Indeed, it's the very nature of faith to do so and with increasing frequency. Jesus the vine didn't say, "I *hope* you bear fruit" or "You *must* bear fruit." He simply said, "You *will* bear fruit" and even added the word *much.* How can children of God still live like children of the devil? How can those who revel in Christ's love react in hate toward those around them? How can those who are remade in God's unselfish image still measure thoughts, words, and deeds with the tiny yardstick of personal selfishness? Though this side of heaven the best of our blossoms still exhibit sin's blight, they grow. When James declares that "faith without deeds is dead," he's reminding us that "no roses means it's not a rose bush" (2:26).

Fertilizer

Leave the watering can in the garage for two weeks and go all season without any fertilizer and see what your rose bush will look like. The sun's suffocating heat and the soil's dwindling nutrients will take their toll.

The comparison again is obvious. The Holy Spirit has a watering can and a bag of fertilizer that we call the gospel. When Jesus declares that "apart from me you can do nothing" (John 15:5), he's reminding us that we need regular feedings not only to blossom but even to remain rose bushes.

So what does my rose bush look like?

Prayer: "Create in me a new heart, Lord,
That gladly I obey your Word.
Oh, let your will be my desire
And with new life my soul inspire." Amen.

(CW 471:3)

The Third Article

_____

"... and kept me in the true faith."

Good thing my father couldn't see it. The strawberry bed he had lavished so much care on was strangled by weeds. The city fathers had purchased our small farm for an industrial park and had let this corner sit idle for several years. When I stopped by out of nostalgia, I was dismayed. No more green, healthy strawberry plants and certainly no more fruit, because no one had cared for the bed.

That's what the heart of faith would look like, suffocated by weeds and stripped bare of fruit, if there were no Holy Spirit to care for it. Last, but in no way least in the work of the Holy Spirit, is his *keeping* us in the true faith.

The weeds keep coming

Think it's exaggeration to claim that without the Holy Spirit's continued work we'd revert to unbelief in a second? Not if we understand who the enemies of faith are and how fiercely they attack us. Let's ask Eve, no longer sinless in a no longer perfect Garden of Eden. "Eve," we wonder, "would you agree with Paul's words to the Christians at Corinth? Was he right when he warned, 'I am afraid that just as Eve was deceived by the *serpent's cunning,* your minds may somehow be led astray from your sincere and pure devotion to Christ' (2 Corinthians 11:3)? What would you have to say to us,

Eve, about the creeping Jenny we call unbelief and how quickly it can root in the heart?"

Or should we interview Judas, if we could find him? "Judas, tell us how it happened. How in heaven's name could you palm those paltry pieces of silver and place that betraying kiss on your Savior's cheek? What would you have to say to us, Judas, about the noxious weed we call 'love of the things of this world' and how it just keeps on growing until faith is forced out of the heart?"

Might we also have a few questions for Simon Peter? "Peter, we know how you cried those bitter tears that night when the rooster crowed and the Savior looked at you. But what brought you to that moment? What kind of weed seed did Satan sow in your heart to make you more concerned about saving your own skin than standing up for your Savior?"

Think it can't happen to us? Think again! Look around at those whose hearts the weeds have taken over: members of our confirmation class, of our own family circles, of those who used to worship with us. Be warned, but above all, be aware of what to do and where to turn—to the Holy Spirit and the gospel he uses to keep on weeding in our hearts.

The Holy Spirit keeps weeding

David could tell us of the Spirit's needed weeding. In words many of us have sung after many a sermon, he prayed: "Create in me a pure heart, O God, and renew a steadfast spirit within me. Do not cast me from your presence or take your Holy Spirit from me. Restore to me the joy of your salvation and grant me a willing spirit, to sustain me" (Psalm 51:10-12). Only the Spirit could pluck the weeds of sin from David's heart and restore the joy of God's salvation to him. For the Spirit's constant presence, he prayed. Are we less needy than David? Don't we learn from him where to turn—to the precious gospel message through which the Spirit pardons our sins and powers our lives for service? Can't we see what will happen to us if we neglect that Word as David did for a while?

Peter could tell us of the Spirit's needed weeding. He advised first-century Christians, "[You] through faith are shielded by God's power until the coming of the salvation that is ready to be revealed in the last time" (1 Peter 1:5). From Peter, who had fallen, comes the warning "Watch out, it could happen to you." But more so from Peter, whom the Lord picked up, comes the assurance "God's power will keep you until it takes you to glory." Only we need to turn to that power. Disconnect the line coming into your meter, and see how long your lights shine. Run the gas tank dry, and see how far your auto rolls. This we can understand. But far more necessary is the realization that a disconnect from the gospel in Word and sacraments has the same effect on our faith and life.

Do we want hearts and lives that are more weed free? Then let's remember who does the weeding and how he does it.

Prayer: "Let not the foe of Christ and man
                 This holy seed remove,
                 But give it root in ev'ry heart
                 To bring forth fruits of love." Amen. (CW 324:2)

The Third Article

"... the holy Christian church, the communion of saints ..."

Our doctor friend in the congregation relaxed by doing woodwork. One Christmas season he surprised us with a boot bench, handcrafted of solid maple. Every time we passed that bench in the parsonage entryway or sat on it to remove our winter boots, we thought of Dr. Ray.

Every time we confess "I believe in the holy Christian church," do we pause to think of the Holy Spirit? The church is his handiwork. The Holy Spirit made and makes it by working in others that which he has worked and works in me.

Put together by the Spirit's toil

"Remember your ABC's," I'd tell the 8th graders when teaching them about the church. The church that we confess in the Third Article is not some structure with a steeple. Nor is it some outward grouping of people gathered in some geographic place. It's <u>A</u>ll <u>B</u>elievers in <u>C</u>hrist. To illustrate this truth, the Creed not only speaks of the "holy Christian church" but goes on without pause to the phrase "the communion of saints." God's church is a "communion," a union or company of people. There's only one such "communion" in his eyes, and it's made up of special people. Not all people, not even all religious people, not even all Lutherans belong to this unique company. Only those who are "saints."

Who might these "saints" be? If we remember that *saint* means "holy," we have an excellent clue. To God's church belong only those who are sinless in his sight. Lest we, knowing well how much we sin daily, fear that this leaves us out in the cold, let's hurry on to the next word. God's church is "Christian." It is built on the only foundation possible, Jesus Christ and him crucified. Only those belong to God's church who, through faith, are clothed with Christ's robe of righteousness. When God looks at such people, he no longer sees their sins, but his Son's righteousness. Though yet sinners, believers in Christ are saints in his sight.

We can't take a census of his church; only God knows each member. He can see where we cannot: into the heart. That's why we call this one church invisible. I can use my passport to prove my US citizenship and my confirmation certificate to prove my congregational membership, but only God can see faith in Jesus, the Savior in my heart.

How come we are numbered among the ABC's? How come we stand along with Adam and Eve, Abraham and Aaron, Moses and Elijah, Peter, James, and John in this select grouping? How come we'll be numbered in that great multitude from every nation, tribe, people, and language before the eternal throne of the Lamb? There's only one answer. It's entirely the handiwork of the Holy Spirit. He "calls, gathers, enlightens, and sanctifies the whole Christian church on earth, and keeps it with Jesus Christ in the one true faith."

Put together by the Spirit's tools

We can't point out who are members of God's church, but we can point out where to find them. If you want a fresh loaf of bread, you stop at the bakery, not the hardware store. If your car needs fuel, you don't head for the barber shop; you head for the gas station. You look for the means that produce the bread and pump the fuel. Likewise, if you want to find believers in Christ, you look for the tools the Holy Spirit uses to work faith.

"From the beginning God chose to save you through the sanctifying work of the Spirit and through belief in the truth. He called you to this *through our gospel,* that you might share in the glory of our Lord Jesus Christ," Paul summarized for the Thessalonians (2 Thessalonians 2:13,14). The tool the Spirit uses to build God's glorious church is the gospel, as he has given it in Word and sacrament. This powerful tool works, even if we can't see it, in the human heart. "So is my word," God promised, "that goes out from my mouth: It will not return to me empty, but will accomplish what I desire and achieve the purpose for which I sent it" (Isaiah 55:11). Where the Word is preached and the sacraments administered, the Spirit is at work, and we can find the church, the ABC's, even if we can't point them out individually.

When church bodies around us have abandoned or try to find substitutes for the Spirit's tools, we still have them. Now let's rededicate ourselves to using the gospel. Only through it does the Spirit work to connect us and others to the holiness of Christ and to craft us into the holy Christian church, the communion of saints.

Prayer: Lord Jesus, may I be counted among those who are members of your church. Amen.

The Third Article

"In the same way he calls, gathers, enlightens, and sanctifies the whole Christian church on earth, and keeps it with Jesus Christ in the one true faith."

I was the only boy in a family of four children. When I couldn't coax my sisters to play ball with me, I resorted to pitching a tennis ball against the hay barn wall. As it bounced back, I became the shortstop fielding the ball. Then I became the first baseman receiving the short-stop's throw ricocheting off the wall. It was much more exciting and complete when the neighborhood kids got together to form teams.

Individuals whom the Spirit has brought to Christ make up God's invisible church. In heaven, they will stand together, revealed as his very own. Here on earth, they look for others like them. They form visible churches to enhance their joy by sharing it and to carry out their work better together. Such visible churches are composed of those who *say* they are believers in Christ. To God's invisible church belong only those who *are* believers. But we'll let God sort out the difference.

Why do we join earthly churches?

If there were no earthly churches, would I be a believer? Certainly my parents could have introduced me to the one who loves the lambs. Perhaps they would also have baptized me and, with this miracle, recorded my name in the book of life. They might even have instructed me, teaching me the Word of Truth for tender youth. But how much better when parents have a church, with people and spiritual leaders around them, to assist them with these important tasks.

Also what would individual believers do when they need an arm around their shoulder because of life's burdens? When their faith needs strengthening and their course needs correction? When they need more than milk for their spiritual diet? How would they "spur one another on toward love and good deeds" (Hebrews 10:24)? How would they "teach and admonish one another with all wisdom" (Colossians 3:16)? How would they be "mutually encouraged by each other's faith" (Romans 1:12)?

How far could individual believers carry Christ's command to "preach the good news to all creation" (Mark 16:15)? How many citizens in their own communities, how many counties in their own state—not to mention countries in their world—could they reach? How many missionaries could they train, send, and support to help them with his work?

Believers are interested in more than bouncing a tennis ball alone against a hay barn wall. That's why they follow the example of the early Christians in the New Testament and join together with others.

What kind of earthly churches do we join?

Believers, however, are careful about what kind of earthly churches they join. No thinking person wants to drink water contaminated with cryptosporidium germs or eat hamburger tainted with E. coli bacteria. They don't want to become sick or, even worse, die. Concerned Christians also want food that is pure. They realize that any adulteration of God's Word, whether through subtraction or addition, poses a danger for their faith. All of Scripture revolves around its central message of God's declaring sinners holy through Christ's saving work. Any chipping away at any teaching eventually leads to contamination of that vital central truth. Realizing this danger, Christians look for a visible church that teaches them " everything [the Savior] commanded" (Matthew 28:20). They hear the Savior command "keep away" from those who would proclaim anything "contrary to the teaching you have learned" (Romans 16:17). And they know why he said it. It was out of deep concern that our souls not become sick and that those exposed to false teaching realize their danger.

When Christians look for a visible church that teaches the pure Word, it's not out of snobbery, as if there are no true believers in Christ in other churches. As long as the gospel is preached in some form, the Spirit will be at work. Rather it's love in capital letters, LOVE for the truth of God's Word, LOVE for our own souls, and LOVE for the souls of others that causes us so to act.

Prayer: Lord, thank you for adding me to your holy church. Help me along with my fellow believers on earth to build your church by sharing your Word. Amen.

The Third Article

"...the forgiveness of sins..."

What can't you live without? "Water," the person burning up in the desert might whisper. "Love," the newly married couple might reply. Now let's ask a second question. What can't you die without? Do you think there would be a quick flow of answers to that question? Or silence?

We cannot live or die without the forgiveness of sins. It's mankind's crucial need in life and death. It's found only in God's gospel, only in his church, only as his Holy Spirit works in the human heart. That's why after we have confessed "I believe in the Holy Spirit, the holy Christian church, the communion of saints," the creed takes us to the "forgiveness of sins."

How it comes

Ever been in a court room and watched the proceedings? The gavel bangs and the verdict is pronounced. Forgiveness, or justification, takes us to the court of heaven. The sinner is the accused; the judge is God. Only God can forgive, for it is against him that all have and do sin. Only he can justify, that is, declare the sinner not guilty.

How can the heavenly judge declare us not guilty? We know what we are. "If you, O LORD, kept a record of sins, O Lord, who can stand?" has to be our confession (Psalm 130:3). "Guilty as charged" is the verdict we deserve. Yet, the heavenly judge acquits us. Not because he is corrupt and sweeps our crimes under the carpet or because he's some indulgent grandpa who winks at our sins. No, he acquits us because he has already paid the penalty for the guilty. His love, as only it could, found a way to satisfy his justice. "God was reconciling the world to himself in Christ, not counting men's sins against them," is Paul's sweet summary (2 Corinthians 5:19). "All our sins on him (Christ) were laid; all our sins by him were paid," is another way of saying it. *Grace* is the word we use to describe this totally undeserved gift of full forgiveness from God.

Like money some gracious benefactor has deposited in the bank, forgiveness of sins is there for every sinner in this world. But only those who draw on the deposit receive the benefit. Faith does not create the forgiveness but receives it. And faith is the tremendous miracle the Holy Spirit works in the human heart. Not only does the Spirit, in the gospel, offer forgiveness to sinners, but also, through the gospel, he works faith to receive it.

In heaven's courtroom, God declares us "not guilty," purely by his grace, for Christ's sake, through faith. Thankful Christians never tire of marveling at and rejoicing in this glorious truth.

What it brings

What happens to those who know that God daily and richly forgives their sins? For them the heavenly judge is no longer someone to hide from in the bushes of life, as fallen Adam and Eve did in the garden. They rejoice in his presence and walk joyously at his side, soaking in the sunshine of his forgiveness.

For them, as they walk at his side, the question is not "Why should I?" but "Lord, what do you want me to do?" The Christian life is not something that needs to be squeezed out of them and that comes only as long as sufficient pressure is kept on them. No, the Christian life is the willing response of a heart that feels God's daily and rich forgiveness of sins.

For them, there is the ability to forgive those who sin against them. Christians forgive family members, fellow church members, next door neighbors—because they believe in the forgiveness of sins. They experience it daily and richly from their heavenly Father and follow his example in dealing with others.

For them, telling others about God's daily and rich forgiveness is not some take-it-or-leave-it proposition but a vital part of their continued existence. Their Savior is also the world's Savior, and the world needs to be told.

For them, there is peace in the hour of death. It's not some feverish tallying up of life's ledger to see if they have achieved the impossible and earned God's forgiveness, but it's a peaceful falling asleep in Jesus' wounds where pardon for their sins abounds.

Are you beginning to understand why we just cannot live or die without the forgiveness of sins?

Prayer: Lord, teach us so to live and to die. For Jesus' sake. Amen.

The Third Article

". . . the resurrection of the body . . ."

Will I ever see him again? Her favorite son had gone off to war. His troop ship had been sunk by torpedoes in the Atlantic. All she had left was a photo of him in his uniform that sat on top of her TV set. And every time I visited this elderly shut-in, she asked the same question. Would she see her son again?

She knew the answer. As a Christian, she believed in the resurrection of the body, both hers and her son's. But she needed the reminder. So do we. We need the work of the Spirit through Word and sacrament to point us forward to the end of it all, the day when we will stand with body and soul reunited in our Father's heaven.

Look ahead with bright eyes

Everybody dies. For some, physical life may stretch beyond the proverbial threescore years and ten; for others less. It makes no difference whether you're a millionaire in a mansion or a homeless person on the street. There are no alternatives, no detours on the road to death. For each of us, life moves relentlessly forward to that moment when the soul leaves the body and goes either to heaven or to hell.

The lifeless form that housed our soul begins immediately to return to dust, regardless of what we do to it. But that's not the end. The tears we shed at the graveside of loved ones are not bitter tears. They are expressions of sorrow over what we have lost—not over what dying Christians gain. Their souls are in heaven at once, and their bodies, to which we do our last labor of love, will one day be there too. Yes is the answer to that shut-in's question. She would see her son again. His body would be lifted from the deep recesses of the sea to be rejoined with his soul for an eternal existence in the place we know as heaven.

So look ahead with bright eyes, fellow believers, made such by the Spirit. In heaven, we'll see our loved ones again in the same bodies we hugged here on earth, though now glorified in ways beyond our imagination. In heaven, our bodies that break down more frequently as the years pile up will be freed of pains. Raised from the grave, those bodies will also be released of all the defects of this life and be like our risen Savior's glorified body. As Luther put it: "We must henceforth learn a new language and speech in talking of death and the grave when we die. It should not be called dying but being sown for the coming summer and that the churchyard or burial mound is not a mound of dead bodies but an acre full of grain, called God's grain, which is to sprout again and to grow more beautifully than any man can comprehend" (Plass, *What Luther Says*, Vol. 1, page 378).

Look ahead with bold eyes

Can we be sure? Who has returned to tell us? Some days we wish we could talk to Lazarus returned from the grave, but none of his words were recorded. Could that be because we have better words? Didn't God tell us that the resurrection of the body will take place? And when God speaks, don't things always happen? Like in the days of creation when he said, "Let there be." Or on the Sea of Galilee when he told the storm, "Be still." Or outside of Nain's gate when he commanded the dead young man, "Arise." "A time is coming," Jesus himself has told us, "when all who are in their graves will hear his voice and come out" (John 5:28,29). God himself has said so and that's good enough for us.

Moreover, God himself has shown us. The path to his Son's tomb contained two sets of footprints, one leading to the tomb and the other away from it. For his Son's grave, there were two doors, one marked "entrance" and the other "exit." The resurrection of Christ is the battering ram that knocks down the walls of our tomb, wherever it may be, and guarantees the springing back to life for our body. The Holy Spirit who has brought us to faith in Christ's resurrection, brings us also to faith in our resurrection. So Paul assures us: "If the Spirit of him who raised Jesus from the dead is living in you, he who raised Christ from the dead will also give life to your mortal bodies through his Spirit, who lives in you" (Romans 8:11).

Because of the Spirit's work, we can answer, "Yes, we shall see each other again." God, help us look forward to that great day, not only with bright eyes but bold eyes.

Prayer: Risen Savior, through your Spirit's work, keep our eyes on your resurrection so that we believe also in ours. Amen.

The Third Article

"... and the life everlasting."

"What kind of work are you in?" people ask as they seek to find out more about you and your occupation. Now if you were to ask the Holy Spirit the same question, what might he say? Do you think his reply would be, "My work is to get people ready to live forever"? That's what the Third Article indicates as it ends with words about life everlasting.

The only life worth having

How do we tell someone about everlasting life? That's like trying to describe an elephant to an Eskimo who has never been near one or a Beethoven symphony to someone who has never heard one of its chords. It's even more difficult than that. For elephants and symphonies are part of this world, but everlasting life is beyond our experience. We who are so bound by the dimensions of time and space, by the ticking of the clock and the square footage of this world, can't begin to fathom what life in heaven will be like.

Perhaps that's why the inspired authors in Scripture often start by telling us what heaven is not. "No more pain," John tells us in Revelation 21:4, and we, who so often wrestle with and weary under pain, can nod somewhat in understanding. "No more death," he also says, and again we, who are shrouded in death's shadow all our days, can take a hint. "No more crying," he adds, no more tears inside our broken hearts or outside on our pillows because of the bumps and bruises, the hurts and hardships of life. In Revelation chapter 7, John points out something else that will be missing in heaven. When he describes the saints in heaven as dressed in white, he's indicating we'll be pure and holy. "No more sin," he's telling us—no more evil heart within to trip us; no more evil world around us to tempt us; no more evil foe to trick us, such as we experience each earthly day.

When Scripture goes on to tell us what heaven will be, understanding becomes even more difficult. How do we wrap our minds around a life that never ends in an eternity that might be described as "God's ever ever land"? How can there be "fulness of joy" when all our life we are so used to having joy and sorrow mixed, pleasure and pain intermingled? What can it be like to be ever with the Lord in a step-by-step walking with him—when on earth we so often stray from his side? And the sight of his loving face? How we've longed for it and wondered what it would be like. Just think—seeing and experiencing with both our body and soul the one loveliest to our eyes, dearest to our heart, most precious to our soul and never having the glorious sight blurred by sin again.

Let shortsighted people waste their lives by limiting them only to this ball of mud. Because of the Spirit's work in our hearts, our eyes are raised and our hearts set on the only life worth having, the everlasting one in heaven.

The only way to have it

Not all people will enjoy everlasting life. Some will experience the opposite. For them it will be everlasting damnation, worse than anything they could ever have imagined. To be locked up in hell and know that it is entirely their own fault. To see not God's smiling face but his back as he turns forever away from them. To wish futilely that after a hundred thousand years, hell's pain would end, but knowing it never will. God preserve us from such an eternity.

In his grace he has. In his love he sent his Spirit to work faith in our hearts so that our names are included in the "whoever" of John 3:16. God so loved the world and sent his Son to die for all sinners, but only "whoever" believes in him will have everlasting life. That's what his Spirit does for us. His work is to get us ready to live forever by bringing us to and keeping us in faith in the only way there is, the Savior Jesus Christ.

Let's not wait until we stand in glory to enjoy the Spirit's gift of everlasting life. Let's show in our daily lives that we know what we have in Christ Jesus. Let's also share with others what we have. After all, that's the reason the Savior still leaves us here once the Spirit has readied us for heaven.

Prayer: Holy Spirit, thank you for faith in Jesus, the only way to heaven. Use us to lead others to the way that they might share everlasting life with us. Amen.

The Ten Commandments

The First Commandment

You shall have no other gods.

What does this mean?

We should fear, love, and trust in God above
all things.

The Second Commandment

You shall not misuse the name of the Lord your God.

What does this mean?

We should fear and love God that we do not use his
name to curse, swear, lie, or deceive, or to use
witchcraft, but call upon God's name in every
trouble, pray, praise, and give thanks.

The Third Commandment

Remember the Sabbath day by keeping it holy.

What does this mean?

We should fear and love God that we do not despise
preaching and his Word, but regard it as holy and
gladly hear and learn it.

The Fourth Commandment

Honor your father and mother, that it may go well with you and that you may enjoy long life on the earth.

What does this mean?

We should fear and love God that we do not dishonor or anger our parents and others in authority, but honor, serve, and obey them, and give them love and respect.

The Fifth Commandment

You shall not murder.

What does this mean?

We should fear and love God that we do not hurt nor harm our neighbor in his body, but help and befriend him in every bodily need.

The Sixth Commandment

You shall not commit adultery.

What does this mean?

We should fear and love God that we lead a pure and decent life in words and actions, and that husband and wife love and honor each other.

The Seventh Commandment

You shall not steal.

What does this mean?

We should fear and love God that we do not take our neighbor's money or property, or get it by dishonest dealing, but help him to improve and protect his property and means of income.

The Eighth Commandment

You shall not give false testimony against your neighbor.

What does this mean?

We should fear and love God that we do not tell lies about our neighbor, betray him, or give him a bad name, but defend him, speak well of him, and take his words and actions in the kindest possible way.

The Ninth Commandment

You shall not covet your neighbor's house.

What does this mean?

We should fear and love God that we do not scheme to get our neighbor's inheritance or house, or obtain it by a show of right, but do all we can to help him keep it.

The Tenth Commandment

You shall not covet your neighbor's wife, workers, animals, or anything that belongs to your neighbor.

What does this mean?

We should fear and love God that we do not force or entice away our neighbor's spouse, workers, or animals, but urge them to stay and do their duty.

The Conclusion

What does God say about all these commandments?

He says, "I, the LORD your God, am a jealous God, punishing the children for the sin of the fathers to the third and fourth generation of those who hate me, but showing love to a thousand generations of those who love me and keep my commandments."

What does this mean?

God threatens to punish all who transgress these commandments. Therefore we should fear his anger and not disobey what he commands.

But he promises grace and every blessing to all who keep these commandments. Therefore we should love and trust in him and gladly obey what he commands.

The Ten Commandments

"You shall have no other gods."

"She's the only one for me." That's why the young man keeps dating her and finally proposes marriage. That's why he's also concerned about following her likes and avoiding her dislikes.

That's what God wants too. He desires people who consider him the only one for them and whose only goal it is to please him. That we might know what our God likes and dislikes, he gave his Ten Commandments. That we might want to follow his will, he gave his Son to redeem us. Having looked at what God's love does for us as outlined in the creed, it's time to turn to the Ten Commandments and look at what he wants us willingly to do for him.

He wants to be our only God

People are by nature incurably religious. The world around them and their consciences within them point irrefutably to the existence of a higher being. Because man without the Word can't know who that God is, he goes about inventing his own. Whether it's the forces of nature around him, the idols crafted by his own hands, or reliance on his own abilities, he has a god. Poor fool! How can an idol of his own creation stand taller than the One who created it? How can the shifting sands of his own intellect or power be reliable concrete for his trust? How can the impersonal, uncaring forces in nature hold him in the palm of their hand?

Careful! When we say "poor fool," we might be pointing the finger also at ourselves. Luther once wrote, "Your god in reality is that around which you entwine your heart and on which you place your confidence" (Plass, *What Luther Says*, Vol. 2, page 541). Perhaps we don't in our blindness bow down to wood and stone. But that doesn't mean we have no idols. When I hold on to my money tighter than to my Master, trust my muscles more than my Maker, respect peoples' opinion more than my Redeemer's, what am I really doing? I'm telling God that he's not the only one, that someone else has the hold on my heart that he alone has the right to have.

He wants to be treated as our only God

Not only does God demand, as he has the right to, that he be our only God, he also asks that we treat him that way. Those three men with hard to pronounce names who were hurled into Nebuchadnezzar's blazing furnace understood this truth (Daniel 3). They revered God so much that they just couldn't think of treating a man-made idol the same way. What had that idol done for them, contrasted to the love God had heaped upon them? Moreover, God had told them in his Word that he wanted the glory given to him, not to idols. Our catechism refers to this giving all glory to God by putting him and his Word above everything else "fearing him above all things."

Those three men understood something else. Their lives were important to them as ours are to us. But not more important than their God. How could they save their skins and sacrifice their God? What kind of love would that show for the true God who had done so much for them, including promising to send the Savior? Our catechism calls this treasuring God above everything else and showing it by following his will as "loving him above all things."

A third truth those three men show us. King Nebuchadnezzar's anger was hot and the furnace's fires even hotter, but the men weren't afraid. Even though those fires promised searing, brutal death, the three men trusted God. Their lives were in his hands, so how could they go wrong? Our catechism calls this relying on God for help more than on anything else as "trusting him above all things."

Guilty? Of course we are! Each of us can write his own "three men in the furnace" scenario, showing with the less dramatic details of our daily life how often we fail to fear, love, and trust God above all things. How in the world are we going to treat God the way he deserves if we can't even begin with this first and foremost commandment, the one that speaks about the state of our mind and heart?

Thank God he rescues us from the fires of hell we deserve. He sent not an angel, but his own Son to pay for our breaking of his First Commandment. Because of Jesus, he still is the only one for us!

Prayer: Lord, thank you for washing us clean from our idolatry. Help us to fear, love, and trust you more each day. Amen.

The Ten Commandments

_____

"You shall not misuse the name of the Lord your God."

"Laura" was the name carved on the tree along the hiking path. Someone had cut a heart into the bark and inside it her name. Made you wonder who she was, what she was like, and who so lovingly had put her name there.

When the Second Commandment speaks of God's name, it refers not only to every name we know him by but everything we know about him from his Word. What a name it is, this name above all other names. Knowing what the true God has done for us, we want to do more than lovingly carve his name on some tree in the woods. We want to give it the highest honor and respect all of our days.

The important meaning of his name

My name is important. It's my exclusive possession, a verbal substitute for me. When it is mentioned, people think of what I look like, what I am, what I do, and what their reaction toward me is. My name is also powerful. It's on the bottom line of checks and on the mortgage papers. My name on those pieces of paper puts my power behind what they represent.

How people use my name is also important for it reveals what they think of me. When my name is spoken in jest or derision, it tells me I don't mean much, if anything, to the speaker. When my name is mispronounced or slurred over, it shows how insignificant I am to them. When people attach honor and respect to my name, it also tells me something.

How much more true it is when it comes to our God. If speech mirrors what's in the heart, then our use of God's name reveals what we think of him. See how naturally this Second Commandment follows upon the First. He who demands that he be our one and only God asks that we show he is by the way we speak about him. When we use names such as "God," "Maker," "Jesus," "Savior," "Spirit," and "Sanctifier" we are speaking more than combinations of consonants and vowels. We are referring to the one more important to us than anyone else in this world. We are also reminding ourselves of what marvelous things he does for us, as his Word reveals. If only we would stop to think of the important meaning of his name each time we use it.

The important use of his name

Who of us would doodle on a picture of our parents or scribble across a photo of our beloved? *Misuse* or stronger words come to mind in describing such behavior. Yet people do even worse with God's holy name and Word. They misuse his name in "cursing," asking the one who would rather bless to send people, animals, or things to hell. They misuse his name in "swearing," asking the one who is truth to witness to their lies or trivial matters. They misuse his name in "witchcraft," turning with their unhealthy inquisitiveness from the one who knows and holds the future to horoscopes, ouija boards, and fortune tellers. They misuse his name in "lying," twisting and turning what he has so clearly spoken in his Word into what they want him to say. They misuse his name in "deceiving," putting over their unbelief the mask of hypocrisy, expecting to fool God as well as their peers.

Guilty? Of course we are! If each night we could listen to a recording of all our speech that day, the words "Forgive us our trespasses" would have added meaning for us. Thank God the blood of Jesus, his Son, purifies us from all our misuses of his precious name. And each day, if we'd remember the proper use of God's name, how much better off we'd be. Like some child calling out for its parent in the middle of the night, so trouble's shadows would drive us to "call upon God's name." Like barren Hannah who prayed for a child, like King David who prayed for protection, like the centurion who prayed for a sick servant, so we'd learn to *pray* in all the affairs and circumstances of life. Like the Samaritan leper who ran down the street shouting out the name of the one who had healed him, so our worship hymns, daily speech, and mission efforts would resound with *praise* for our helper. Like the grateful woman who anointed his feet with precious perfume, so we'd *give thanks* by pouring our daily thoughts, words, and deeds over our Savior's feet.

God in grace has carved his name, the one above all other names, on our hearts. God, help us in response to hold that name high above all others in our lives.

Prayer: Dear Lord, may I never forget to give you praise and glory for all the great and wonderful things you have done. Amen.

The Ten Commandments

_____

"Remember the Sabbath day by keeping it holy."

Sometimes shadows can be useful. If, for example, I'm relaxing on the patio behind my house on a sunny summer afternoon listening to the ball game on the radio, and I hear a car door slam out on the driveway, I don't have to leave my chair. I can watch the corner of the house for the shadow of the person coming to learn something about him. The shadow tells me something about the height, size, and gender of the one coming. Of course, once the visitor has rounded the house corner, I look directly at him instead of the shadow.

God's Sabbath law for his Old Testament people was like that shadow. It told them somewhat of the Savior who was coming around the corner of the New Testament. As they rested from physical work on the Sabbath, they were to look ahead to the one coming to bring them rest from the sins that wearied their souls.

The rest God offers

The real Sabbath is eternal rest. It's undisturbed fellowship with God. It's being at peace with him. It's being able to walk and talk again with God as Adam and Eve did in the garden, before sin brought fear and death and judgment. And it's being able to look forward with confidence to the perfect walk with him in heaven.

This heavenly rest comes only through Jesus. Because of the Savior's full payment for sin's debt, man can once again stand before God in peace. God offers this beautiful rest for sin-troubled souls in his Word. Nowhere else can mankind find Christ's rest. Only in the Word is forgiveness offered, and only through the Word does the Spirit work faith in the sinner's heart to receive it.

For God's Old Testament people, the Third Commandment did indeed mandate a day of rest for their bodies. Even more though was it intended to raise their eyes in expectant faith to the Savior whose coming would bring rest for their souls. In this sense the Sabbath day was a shadow of Christ. Now that our rest bringer has come, we look no longer at the shadow but directly at him. For us as New Testament Christians, the Third Commandment speaks not about what to do with a day that was only a shadow but with God's Word that brings true rest for our souls. For us this commandment is an invitation to think back to Eden and what life was once like, and to think ahead to eternity and what life will be like because of Jesus.

The rest we need

One thing kept the downed Air Force pilot going during his months in the Vietcong prison camp. It was the last letter from his wife that he had tucked in his flight-suit pocket before takeoff. Again and again he read it until its edges were tattered and the creases torn. We've received a love letter from our God. In it he tells us about the relationship that he wants with us and has made possible for us through the Savior, Jesus. How are we using his Word? Are we "holding it sacred," more dear to us than that aviator's letter? Do we show how precious is the book divine by the way we "gladly hear and learn it"? When it's time for public worship, do we rejoice with those who say "let us go to the house of the LORD" (Psalm 122:1)? In our personal daily devotions, do we say with Jeremiah, "When your words came, I ate them; they were my joy and my heart's delight" (15:16)? Few of us would say that we don't need the rest God has prepared for us in Jesus. Few of us would say that his Word, in which that rest is offered, isn't precious to us. Hopefully our actions say the same thing.

Almost every Sunday an elderly believer would voice his concern to me. Sig had refused to join the congregation until after his wife's death. Then he came because he wanted to find the peace she had shown in her struggle with the cancer that ended her life. Walking out of church on Sunday, he would lament to me, "Why was I so foolish? Why did I wait so long? Why did I cheat myself out of so much?" "Gladly," Luther said, "Gladly hear and learn it." Sig agreed. He knew what he had missed and how much he needed it. And he knew where to find Christ's precious rest for his soul—in the Word.

Prayer: Lord, "Let your Word e'er be my pleasure and my heart's most precious treasure." Amen. (CW 283:1)

The Ten Commandments

"Honor your father and mother, that it may go well with you and that you may enjoy long life on the earth."

Forsooth. How many still know that word? Or how about *forthwith* or *perchance.* Such words are seldom used anymore in our changing English language. Then there are other words that are used everyday, but seem little understood. Like the words *authority* and *respect* or, to put them together, respect for authority.

It's interesting that God begins the Second Table of his Commandments, the one that speaks about showing love to him by showing love to our fellow man, with a commandment that deals with authority and respect. Let's see why.

Those under authority

If only we could see who stands behind those who have authority over us. The Fourth Commandment starts with father and mother, those closest and most basic for us, but doesn't stop there. With its command to honor those in authority, it extends also to other spheres of life, such as the church, school, and government.

Notice the commandment demands "honor" toward those in authority. Love we are to show toward all, but honor asks for more. Honor refers to recognition of, respect for, and proper response to the authority of a superior. Where do they obtain such authority? Do we honor our parents because we owe our lives to them?

Because they are stronger and wiser than us as children? Because they take good care of us? Or because they are God's representatives through whom he exercises authority over us and channels his blessings to us?

As Christians we know the answer. Parents and presidents are flawed. Teachers and pastors may make mistakes and mismanage their authority. But it's still God who puts them there. They are his representatives, his "stand-ins," his "baby-sitters" over us. No matter what their warts and wrinkles may be, a gracious God wants to channel his blessings to us through them. A government, even though it be humanistic, keeps basic law and order. An employer, even though he be self-serving, puts food on the table. A teacher, even though he be antifamily, imparts basic skills. Because they are God's representatives and channel his blessings to us, we honor, serve, and obey them. Only when they command something contrary to what God has said, do we refuse to follow. When we honor his visible representatives, we are really honoring the invisible Lord.

By connecting a promise with this commandment, God shows us how vital for the well-being of our home and society he considers honor for those in authority. Luther explains, "This, then, is the fruit and the reward, that whoever keeps this commandment will enjoy good days, happiness, and prosperity. On the other hand, the penalty for him who disobeys it is that he will perish sooner and never be happy in life. For, in the Scriptures, to have long life means not merely to grow old but to have everything that pertains to long life—health, wife and child, livelihood, peace, good government, etc., without which this life can neither be heartily enjoyed nor long endure" (Tappert, *Book of Concord*, page 383).

Those in authority

What an awesome responsibility to be God's "stand-in." As parents—to hold in our hands a new life and be responsible for shaping it, not only for earth but eternity. As governing officials—to make decisions always and only for the well-being of the citizens of the land. As pastors—to feed the flock of God with his Word and be answerable for each soul in their care. As teachers—to help shape growing intellect and equip future generations for productive lives. Those whom God has placed in authority gain honor by showing genuine concern for the well-being of those under their authority. Authority is not a club to wield powerfully, but a responsibility to weigh prayerfully.

Thank the loving Father for his Son, Jesus! He put aside heavenly authority to bring us eternal gain. He followed his Father's will perfectly, even to the rough wood of the cross and the raging fires of hell, that we who so often dishonor, disrespect, and disregard authority might look forward with delight to heaven. While still on earth as his pardoned children, whether under or in authority, we can show our delight by the way we deal with each other.

Prayer: Heavenly Father, help me in love to honor my earthly superiors so that I will be obedient to you. In Jesus' name. Amen.

The Ten Commandments

"You shall not murder."

Name your most precious earthly possession. Is the answer "Jesus"? Without the Savior what do we really have? How about another answer? Wouldn't it have to be "life"? God seems to think so. In the Fifth Commandment, he places a protective shield around life, both our own and our neighbor's. "Hands off," he says. "Don't hurt nor harm," he commands. And for good reason. For there's an important connection between the gift of Jesus and the gift of life.

God gives life

Life comes from God. He "breathed into his [Adam's] nostrils the breath of life, the and man became a living being," the sacred record reminds us (Genesis 2:7). Through the miracle of reproduction, God still creates life. Though man can describe this miracle, he cannot make it happen. Many a childless couple can tell us that.

Moreover, God preserves life. The dinner table prayer, "The eyes of all look to you, and you give them their food at the proper time," echoes this truth (Psalm 145:15). God clothes us and feeds us. He keeps our hearts beating and lungs breathing. He keeps disease away from us or heals us when it comes—until he wants our life to end. "My times are in your hands," the psalmist correctly states (31:15). Those who cannot give life have no right to end it. When they do, they take what comes from God and belongs to him.

Most important of all, God has a sacred purpose for life. The old expression "life is what you make it" isn't true. It's what God made it. God grants life as the precious time of grace for each individual to be brought to faith in his Son. "I have come that they may have life, and have it to the full," the Savior declares (John 10:10). It's as simple and precious as that. Life is the time God grants each of us to receive the full life, the eternal life, the life that never ends in Jesus. No man has the right to shorten that precious time—either for himself or someone else.

God guards life

Yet what do we find all around us? What God begins, man ends. What God heals, man hurts. What God has sacred purpose for, man sinfully perverts. The second sin recorded in Scripture is that of one brother killing another; and it hasn't stopped today. Thus, a loving God put a protective fence around his precious gift of life, even to the point of requiring the government to end the life of the murderer who wantonly jumps over that fence.

It's not just the act of murder to which the commandment speaks. Peter wore Cain's sandals when, in the shadows of Gethsemane, he sliced off the servant's ear. So do we when reckless actions, thoughtless deeds, or neglect of duty cause others harm. Joseph's brothers wore those same shoes when they cruelly sold their detested brother into slavery and coldheartedly caused their aged father, Jacob, to mourn. So do we when our tongue, like some sharp stiletto, draws invisible blood and leaves emotional gashes. There's more. "Anyone who hates his brother is a murderer," John, the apostle of love, declares firmly (1 John 3:15). In the eyes of the one who guards life, "looks do kill," and he will hold us accountable for bilious thoughts and belligerent feelings. So precious is the individual's time of grace in the eyes of the one who gives it.

"I was hungry and you gave me something to eat . . . I needed clothes and you clothed me" (Matthew 26:35,36), Jesus will tell his own on the Last Great Day. See how closely he connects love for our fellow man with love for him. When we aid those in need, regardless of who they may be or how they may have treated us, we are dealing also with the one behind them as Creator and Redeemer. He wants them to be readied for heaven, and he wants us to help guard their precious time of grace by befriending them in every bodily need.

Guilty? Of course we are. We haven't loved our neighbor as ourselves. If we did, we'd take more seriously God's charge to share with our neighbor the eternal life that is found only in Jesus. We'd even take more seriously the concern for our own soul and more richly use the gospel through which the Spirit brings that life.

Time to say it again—thank God for Jesus. Cleansed by his blood, covered by his grace, we have in him real life, full life, life that never ends.

Prayer: Gracious Lord, thank you for the life that now is and that which is to come. Guide me in following the Savior's example in helping those in need. Amen.

The Ten Commandments

"You shall not commit adultery."

Think marriage is important to God? Wasn't it he who instituted it in the Garden of Eden by bringing Eve to Adam that two might become one flesh? Wasn't it God, come in the flesh, who performed his first miracle at a wedding celebration in Cana? And wasn't it his Spirit who, through Paul, compared the relationship between husband and wife to the union between Christ and the church? To safeguard that which he had so graciously given and which is so obviously important to him, God set down his Sixth Commandment.

A lifelong union of love

"Stop, look, and listen before you cross the tracks of marriage," one of my professors said. Good advice—for once entered, marriage is to be lifelong. "What God has joined together, let man not separate," Jesus commanded (Matthew 19:6). True, sinful people may and do tamper with this lifelong union of love. Swinging the club of selfishness, man shatters this union through unfaithfulness or wilful desertion. Flitting like a bee from blossom to blossom, he cancels out and civil authorities concur, even granting "no-fault" divorces. But that doesn't make sin right! The lasting bruises and painful scars left on all involved in a marriage's breakup show God's wisdom in wanting marriage to be a lasting relationship like that of the church with Christ.

God, who instituted marriage, wants it also to be a life-long union of love and honor for each other. With this gift he intended to bless, not blight mankind. He wanted this union to be a mountaintop of happiness, not a lowland of hurt, for the men and women he created. With man as the head and woman as the heart, earthly marriage was to be a foretaste of the bliss awaiting believers with Christ in heaven's wedding feast. When a husband leads—tying himself with tender cords of love to his wife and thinking in loving concern about her needs first—he's a picture, though faint, of Christ, the heavenly Bridegroom. When a wife follows—leaning trustingly on her husband and looking to him with tender regard—she's a picture, though faint, of Christ's bride, the church. That was God's intention when he brought Eve to Adam in the garden. Because we no longer wear God's image as our wedding garment, we need his commandment to guide us as we seek to follow his will concerning marriage. Even more so do we need his Son to save us when we fail.

A pure and decent life of love

No, the unmarried are not off the hook. Since God gave the precious gift of sexuality to all, this commandment speaks to all, both married and unmarried. When God directs us to use sexual desire only within the framework of marriage, it's for our own good. As with all his commandments, his intention is to protect us. Marriage provides opportunity for expression of the total oneness between a man and a woman and protection for the children who may result from their union. Free and easy sex outside of marriage brands man as little more than an animal and as a sinner in God's eyes.

Not only do impure actions adulterate human hearts, so do impure words and thoughts. Like burning sparks from hell's engine, salacious stories and offensive jokes can light unholy fires along life's tracks. Speaking and listening to such things lend tongues and ears that belong to God to the devil. Such words also affect others and reflect on us and the Savior we claim to follow. Behind speech stands the heart. What we say and do usually depends on what we are thinking. So God judges also the thought. "Anyone who looks at a woman lustfully has already committed adultery with her in his heart," said the Lord Jesus (Matthew 5:28). He who sees all looks also into the hidden depths of our hearts. That heart is like a cage with paper bars holding the lion of our sinful nature in. Why say or think, read or watch, get involved in or go along with anything that might cause it to lunge against those bars and break out.

So what's the Christian to do? We have to live in a world that uses sex to sell, that portrays sex down to the last panting detail in its publications and productions, that disguises sexual innuendo as bright comedy. Swimming in such a polluted river, how can we avoid swallowing more than a mouthful, not to mention going under? Our chief defense is the Word. It refreshes in our hearts the will of God and the story of the Redeemer's love. It points out God's way and provides the power to walk it. It offers pardon when we fail and power to keep on trying. The more his Word fills our hearts with his great love for us in Christ, the more our lives will respond with Joseph, "How then could I do such a wicked thing and sin against God?" (Genesis 39:9).

Prayer: Dear Lord Jesus, help me to be clean in what I think and say and do that I might serve you. Amen.

The Ten Commandments

"You shall not steal."

See the connection? In the Fifth Commandment, God safeguarded the existence of life. In the Sixth Commandment, the continuation of life. And now in the Seventh Commandment, the means for sustaining life. If there had been no fall into sin in Eden's Garden, there'd be no need for the Seventh Commandment. Instead, in love we'd be using earth's stores to sustain ourselves and share with others. But sin changed love into greed and sharing into selfishness.

God gives me mine and my neighbor his

God gives to each what he wants to. To my neighbor he gives his share, and to me he gives mine. What he gives to my neighbor is not mine, and what he gives to me is not my neighbor's—though all still belong to God. The deed to all still carries God's name. But each of us is responsible for what we have received. It is not for me to compare and complain because God may have given my neighbor more than me. My task is to use what God has given me and to keep my hands off what God has given my neighbor.

And that's the problem. There's too much of the thief in each of us. If all who steal were to have their photos stapled up in the post office, we'd have to look for bricks to enlarge the walls. You don't think so? Then consider—not just the gun-wielding thug steals, so does the worker who gives as little effort as possible on the job. Not just the sly-fingered pickpocket steals, so does the student who copies someone else's work. Not just the overcharging merchant steals, so does anyone who seeks gain at another's expense. Not just the church member who brings only a pittance to the Lord steals, so does the one who closes his eyes to a neighbor's needs. How can God, to whom all belongs, stand to look at what we do to each other?

Even more, how can he stand to look at the human heart? That's where all stealing starts. Stealing involves not only possessions but the heart's attitude toward God and our fellow man. The human heart can't find it in itself to trust the giver of all good things, but relies instead on what has been given—worrying that it is not enough and always wanting more. Like some spider, the sinful heart spins its greedy web in which it seeks to entangle what God has given to someone else. "What is mine is mine and what is yours is yours" becomes "what is yours is mine too"—and is not satisfied until "all is mine." Even then, there is little satisfaction, for instead of owning all, the thief discovers, to his folly, that it owns him.

God wants me to use mine and to help my neighbor use his

What's the solution for the stealing heart? Zacchaeus, the tree-climbing tax collector, can show us. He wanted to see Jesus. That's why he, short of stature, climbed the tree in Jericho that day. By God's grace he did more than see Jesus. Jesus saw him and reached for him and forgave him and changed him. Then Zacchaeus was ready to give half of his goods to the poor and restore fourfold what he had stolen. Those who stand in the sunshine of God's forgiving love reflect that giving love to others. As God has loved them, they seek to love their neighbor. Their concern shifts from getting to giving, from stealing to sharing, from hurting to helping.

What does this say about feeding my family, filing my taxes, filling my offering envelopes, feeling for the needy? What does this say about being a good employer or employee, a good neighbor, a good citizen? What does this say about praying for others, promoting their interests, providing help when they need it? And what does this say about using the goods God has entrusted to me to spread the message of salvation? What greater help can we offer to someone than that which readies his soul for eternity?

Do you remember that a thief was crucified with Jesus? That thief belonged on his cross because of his crimes. But do you remember that Jesus talked to that thief and promised him paradise? Doesn't the fact that the dying Savior would talk to a thief and promise him heaven say something to us? It should. For today the same Savior says to each one of us: "I will make a new person out of you. I will drain the greed out of your heart and life and teach you to love others. I will forgive you your sins, also the sins of stealing. And I will bring you to paradise." It's time today for us thieves to thank Jesus again.

Prayer: "In sickness, sorrow, want, or care
        May we each other's burdens share;
        May we, where help is needed, there
        Give help as though to you." Amen.

(CW 499:5)

The Ten Commandments

"You shall not give false testimony against your neighbor."

The gift of speech brings with it much joy. What if we had no ability to say "I love you" or "I care"? What if there'd be no familiar voice on the other end of the long-distance phone call, no first word from a grandchild for our ears to hear? Much sunshine would be lost if the gift of speech were gone. Unfortunately, speech isn't always used to spread sunshine. At times it can fall like hail, denting a reputation, or burn like the desert sun, damaging a good name. Because a good name is a possession people can ill afford to lose and seldom regain, God has set down this commandment.

Destructive speech

Look at what sin did to man's use of God's gift of speech. After the fall Adam used this gift, not to offer praise but instead to offer an excuse to his Maker. Toward his wife it was no longer words of affection but words of accusation. A brief glance into the sin shadows of our own lives verifies what we have seen in Eden. For us too sin has perverted the tongue, as James put it, into "a restless evil, full of deadly poison" (3:8). Like some restless snake, speech slithers around, darting and striking without warning, puncturing and paralyzing reputations with its poison.

Need some specifics? Luther offers them as he unfolds God's commandment with the words "tell lies about our neighbor, betray him, or give him a bad name." With the words "false testimony," God couched his commandment in the language of the courts, but Luther shows it covers the whole field of communication with or about our neighbor. Though Luther speaks of telling lies, betraying, giving a bad name, it's really all the same, just from a different viewpoint. He's speaking of any use of speech, whether it tells a lie or the truth, that is intended to damage a fellow human being's reputation. Sometimes it's telling lies in the courtroom in order to help the guilty or frame the innocent. Sometimes it's gossiping about another, with the mistaken notion that tearing him down builds us up. Doesn't that word *gossip* seem to hiss out the smallness of this sin? Sometimes it's greasing the skids with flattery, as we sweet-talk someone into giving us what we want. Sometimes it's revealing another's sins when it would be far better to conceal them. But always it's trying to damage his reputation.

Why do we do such things? It's not just "tongue trouble" but "heart trouble." The sin in Eden's garden changed not only our vertical relationship with God but also the horizontal one with our neighbor. When sin exiles God from the human heart, our neighbor also loses his worth. When the heart regards God as a nobody, how can our neighbor be somebody? When God's name means little or nothing, what's in a neighbor's name?

Guilty? Of course we are. It's time again to plead in penitence, "God, be merciful to me, a sinner." God will hear and answer. His own living Word of love he placed into a stable and pierced on a cross to cleanse us also from the sins of the tongue. As he plants Christ in our hearts, he also trains our tongues, so that we can use them to help our neighbor.

Constructive speech

Tamed and trained by Christ, the tongue talks up for our neighbor's good. When wicked King Saul spoke ill of David, Jonathan reminded his father of the good that David had done for Israel in slaying Goliath. When David had committed adultery and murder and all Israel knew about it, the prophet Nathan went face-to-face with his king, seeking and succeeding in leading him to repentance's road. When's the last time we scotched some gossip by speaking well about the one being scorched? When's the last time we put the kindest spin on another's actions toward us—instead of trumping up something less than noble? When's the last time we hurried in love to one who had sinned against us—instead of harboring resentment against him and heralding to others what he had done? There's much for us as Christians to do with God's gift of speech, so much that there's no time left for foolishness.

We believe in the one who said of himself, "I am the truth." We follow him whose filled cross and emptied tomb guarantees victory over Satan, "the father of lies." What better way of showing this than speaking the truth with one another?

Prayer: "Keep me from saying things
That later need recalling;
Grant that no idle words
May from my lips be falling,
But then, when in my place
I must and ought to speak,
My words grant pow'r and grace
Lest I offend the weak." Amen. (CW 459:3)

The Ten Commandments

"You shall not covet your neighbor's house."
"You shall not covet your neighbor's wife, workers, animals, or anything that belongs to your neighbor."

"It's your heart," the doctor explains to the patient. Cholesterol has corroded vital vessels and restricted blood flow to the point that, without surgery, death will result. "It's your heart," the Lord also diagnoses, looking at the spiritual condition of all mankind. Only with mankind's heart trouble, corrective surgery like angioplasty or bypass procedures won't do it. More like a transplant is in place. Let's listen carefully as he who began his commandments with one demanding a heart of perfect fear, love, and trust for him, now ends with two commandments taking us deep into the recesses of the human heart.

The cause of covetousness

"You shall not covet," God demands in these two commandments, using a word that means to want something he does not see fit to give us. Though wanting and working for things is not wrong and surely can be commended, sin comes in when God says no. Because the sinful heart still wants, it reaches for a neighbor's house, spouse, workers, animals—anything. Many times that sinful heart covers up its schemes with a show of right, rouging sin's pockmarks with the blush of legitimacy. Like Ahab who craved another man's vineyard and covered his covetousness by claiming it as royal right after the owner had been stoned. Or like David who lusted for another man's wife and legalized his sin later by marrying her. But it was still sin in God's eyes— sin both against the neighbor and against him.

With these two commandments, God slices open the human heart and shows where such sins begin. His words "Do not covet" remind us that we don't become sinners when we sin. It's the other way around—we sin because we are sinners. Our sinful hearts are the cause—the committed sin is the result. And Satan knows just how to play to that diseased heart. He who once unsuccessfully tempted Christ with all the power, possessions, and pleasure of this world can scale down his offer to us, because we settle for so much less. The world pitches in with Satan as it coaches our sinful heart to dissatisfaction with what we have, desire for what someone else has, and doing what we need to do to get it. Even if we are successful in preventing the deed, the thought is still sin. Though the world claims that "it's not the thought, but the deed" or that "it's okay to look, but don't touch," God's words are very clear about how he views coveting.

What do we see when we look into our hearts? More important, what does God see when he looks there? We don't like the answer. We can't do anything about our condition. But God in his grace did and does.

The cure for covetousness

The righteous Lord claims rightly, "The soul that sins shall die," but then the loving Lord, with one death, took care of that penalty for all. The righteous Lord demands correctly, "Be holy because I am holy," but then the loving Lord, with one life, prepared that holiness for all. When we look into the human heart, as these two commandments force us to do, we can only despair. When we look into the divine heart, as the gospel bids us to do, we can only rejoice. See what God has done for us in Christ Jesus! He sent his Son to earth to live for us a life totally untainted by covetousness or any other sin. He sent his Son to earth to totally pay for our covetousness and all our other sins. In God's great love for us in Christ, we have the cure for the human heart.

When a gracious God creates a pure heart in us and restores to us the joy of his salvation, he also makes us content. Eyes that see Jesus' hands stretched out in payment for sin see those same hands stretched out in blessing. Hearts that trust God's love in Christ for cleansing souls from every stain trust that same love to freely offer our bodies everything necessary. Contentment is not a human production. It's God's work in us as he keeps our eyes fastened on Jesus.

Someday the heavenly physician will look at us and say: "It's your heart, the heart of faith I have transplanted in you. Come inherit the kingdom prepared for you."

Prayer: Dear Lord, lead me to love you above all things and to do your will. Through Jesus, my all in all. Amen.

The Ten Commandments

"He says, 'I, the LORD your God, am a jealous God, punishing the children for the sin of the fathers to the third and fourth generation of those who hate me, but showing love to a thousand generations of those who love me and keep my commandments.'"

"That's what *you* think!" "That's what *you* say!" We've all heard and used such expressions to indicate doubt about what someone says. When the Lord God speaks, there can be no uncertainty or unclarity. He's a "jealous" God, one who always says what he means and means what he says. Of this sure truth, he reminds us in the conclusion to his commandments.

He is serious about his threats

It's no coincidence that the commandments end as they began, with reference to "the LORD, your God." The First Commandment directed us to have only him as our God. All the way through the commandments, we heard the Lord our God speaking to us and asking us to follow out of fear and love to him. Now he concludes by once more directing us to him as "the LORD your God." Do we hear what he's telling us? Those are *his* commandments telling us what *he* wants us to do. To follow those commands is to follow *him*. To disobey them is to disobey *him*. And to disobey him is to bring down upon ourselves *his* sure punishment. That's what his word "jealous" tells us. It reminds us the Lord our God is not like some inconsistent parent who threatens and threatens, but then fails to follow through. He will punish if we disobey.

Sinners listen with squeamish ears to such a threat. They'd much rather delude themselves into thinking: "God's not serious. This sin doesn't really count. I can squeak by." But a God who sees every sin, holds the sinner accountable for every sin, and punishes every sin is a portrait we don't readily hang on our family room walls. So serious is the Lord God about sin that he threatens to punish "children for the sin of the fathers to the third and fourth generation of those who hate" him. Sin is hating God, and parents who hate God model such action for their children. The result is that such children often walk in the unbelieving, impenitent shoes of their parents.

But don't the wicked often prosper in this world? Aren't the evildoers frequently at the top of the heap? Just wait. We often can't see the inward anguish of a conscience troubled by God's wrath—such as with Judas. We can sometimes see the outward calamity that God sends—such as with Cain, whose reward for murder was to wander as a marked man the rest of his life. We don't want to see the fires of hell nor join the impenitent there, as they are completely cut off from God in never-ending torment. But let's make no mistake about it: "the LORD your God is a consuming fire, a jealous God" (Deuteronomy 4:24).

He is serious about his promises

The Lord our God is just as serious when he promises to show love to a thousand generations of those who love him and keep his commandments. In fact, if we do our math, we can tell that he would much rather bless than punish, as his reference to a "thousand generations" assures us. To understand this promise, we need to focus on him, not on us. It's not as if we can make claim on God's blessings if we keep such and such and so many of his commandments. What God asks us to do is our duty. Doing our duty earns us nothing from him—not to mention that when we try to do our duty, we still fail frequently. When God promises to bless, it's because of his love. Every blessing he sends on obedient children who try to walk the way of his commandments is undeserved. See how the focus in this blessing is on the Lord our God. Without his love we can't even begin to keep his commandments, because we'd have no faith. Because of his love, however, we can expect his blessings when we try.

We don't see such blessings? Just stop and think. What does it mean to be able to pray each night to "forgive us our trespasses" and then fall asleep in peace while the world around us has no rest? What does it mean—as a believing husband or wife, parent or child, employer or employee—to live in contentment and satisfaction while the world around us scraps with one another and scrapes for things? What does it mean to hold up under trial and handle trouble—while the world around us frets and fears? What does it mean to live with the certainty of heaven while the world around us shakes in uncertainty? No blessings? Count them one by one, and thank the Lord our God for his undeserved love in giving them to unworthy children like us.

When the Lord our God speaks, we don't reply, "That's what you think!" or "That's what you say!" By his grace we know he means it, and we are glad.

Prayer: Heavenly Father, lead me to repentance for my sins and to rejoicing for your love and mercy to me. In Jesus' name, Amen.

The Lord's Prayer

The Address

Our Father in heaven.

What does this mean?

With these words God tenderly invites us to believe that he is our true Father and that we are his true children, so that we may pray to him as boldly and confidently as dear children ask their dear father.

The First Petition

Hallowed be your name.

What does this mean?

God's name is certainly holy by itself, but we pray in this petition that we too may keep it holy.

How is God's name kept holy?

God's name is kept holy when his Word is taught in its truth and purity and we as children of God lead holy lives according to it. Help us to do this, dear Father in heaven! But whoever teaches and lives contrary to God's Word dishonors God's name among us. Keep us from doing this, dear Father in heaven!

The Second Petition

Your kingdom come.

What does this mean?

God's kingdom certainly comes by itself even without our prayer, but we pray in this petition that it may also come to us.

How does God's kingdom come?

God's kingdom comes when our heavenly Father gives his Holy Spirit, so that by his grace we believe his holy Word and lead a godly life now on earth and forever in heaven.

The Third Petition

Your will be done on earth as in heaven.

What does this mean?

God's good and gracious will certainly is done without our prayer, but we pray in this petition that it may be done among us also.

How is God's will done?

God's will is done when he breaks and defeats every evil plan and purpose of the devil, the world, and our sinful flesh, which try to prevent us from keeping God's name holy and letting his kingdom come. And God's will is done when he strengthens and keeps us firm in his Word and in the faith as long as we live. This is his good and gracious will.

The Fourth Petition

Give us today our daily bread.

What does this mean?

God surely gives daily bread without our asking, even to all the wicked, but we pray in this petition that he would lead us to realize this and to receive our daily bread with thanksgiving.

What, then, is meant by daily bread?

Daily bread includes everything that we need for our bodily welfare, such as food and drink, clothing and shoes, house and home, land and cattle, money and goods, a godly spouse, godly children, godly workers, godly and faithful leaders, good government, good weather, peace and order, health, a good name, good friends, faithful neighbors, and the like.

The Fifth Petition

Forgive us our sins, as we forgive those who sin against us.

What does this mean?

We pray in this petition that our Father in heaven would not look upon our sins or because of them deny our prayers; for we are worthy of none of the things for which we ask, neither have we deserved them, but we ask that he would give them all to us by grace; for we daily sin much and surely deserve nothing but punishment.

So we too will forgive from the heart and gladly do good to those who sin against us.

The Sixth Petition

Lead us not into temptation.

What does this mean?

God surely tempts no one to sin, but we pray in this petition that God would guard and keep us, so that the devil, the world, and our flesh may not deceive us or lead us into false belief, despair, and other great and shameful sins; and though we are tempted by them, we pray that we may overcome and win the victory.

The Seventh Petition

But deliver us from evil.

What does this mean?

In conclusion, we pray in this petition that our Father in heaven would deliver us from every evil that threatens body and soul, property and reputation, and finally when our last hour comes, grant us a blessed end and graciously take us from this world of sorrow to himself in heaven.

The Doxology

For the kingdom, the power, and the glory are yours now and forever. Amen.

What does this mean?

We can be sure that these petitions are acceptable to our Father in heaven and are heard by him, for he himself has commanded us to pray in this way and has promised to hear us. Therefore we say, "Amen. Yes, it shall be so."

The Lord's Prayer

"Our Father in heaven."

How often haven't we prayed it? In our family circle and in congregational worship. In times of joy and times of trouble. For good reason. First, because it is our Lord's Prayer, taught by him—not just once, but twice (Matthew 6, Luke 11). Second, because it covers all our needs, both of soul and body. Because we use it so frequently, however, we might be tempted to slide over its few words and lose sight of its rich meaning.

Our *Father*

"Father," Jesus teaches us to call him. Is this because he who formed Adam out of the dust of the ground has also framed us in our mothers' wombs? Of course—he who flings the stars into space and confines the mighty oceans to their channels creates and preserves every human being on earth. But that's not the Father to whom Jesus bids us pray. How could we? Because of Adam's sin, our connection with the almighty, holy God has been severed, and we dare not call him Father.

With *Father,* Jesus has something far greater in mind. "You are all sons of God by faith in Christ Jesus," Paul explains (Galatians 3:26). What a Father he is, one whose love drove him to send his only Son to become our brother and restore us again as his sons and daughters. Never will we cease marveling at "how great is the love the Father has lavished on us, that we should be called children of God!" (1 John 3:1). "For believers only," Jesus marks his prayer by using that word *Father.* Only believers trust God as their loving Father to whom they can come with confidence and peace.

Our Father

Surely it wouldn't be wrong for us to pray "My Father in heaven . . . give *me* today my daily bread . . . forgive *me* my sins." Yet that's not how Jesus taught us to pray. Through sin, mankind lost not only the heavenly Father but also his fellow man. Not only did Adam run away from his Father as from an angry judge, but he also leveled the blaming finger at his wife. God sent his Son, Jesus, to bring back both the fatherhood of God and the brotherhood of man. Those who know the Father pray not in narrow concern only for themselves but in wider concern for all those of the household of faith.

So it's "our" Father as we pray in *concern* for our spouse, our parents, our children, our pastors and teachers, our people, the healthy for the sick and the sick for the healthy, the believers around us whom we can name and the nameless ones thousands of miles away. There's also *comfort* in that word *our.* Across the world, every time a believer uses this prayer, he's praying for me and asking God to grant me what I need for body and soul. Nor do we want to ignore the *challenge* in the word *our.* What about the billions who don't know our loving Father? I know what I have as a member of his family, so I want to do all I can to direct others to that family.

Our Father *in heaven*

What a contrast between fathers on earth and our Father "in heaven." Many earthly fathers try to love with a tender and unselfish love, but there are places their love can't travel and problems their love can't solve. There are also mistakes their love can make—and the grave finally silences their love. Not so with our Father in heaven. "Our God is in heaven; he does whatever pleases him," the psalmist announced (115:3). "Nothing is impossible with God," the angel answered Mary (Luke 1:37). He "is able to do immeasurably more than all we ask or imagine," Paul assured the Ephesians (3:20). A heavenly Father with heavenly power can and will take good care of his children.

Nor does the Father in heaven ever make a mistake. When it seems so—if what has come our way seems heavy and hard—it's time to look up again to the one who sends it. More than any earthly father, he knows what diet is needed to tone faith's muscles and what rain is needed to help faith's flower flourish. "Keep your eyes not on what is sent, but who sends it," Jesus would remind us with the words "our Father in heaven."

"Our Father in heaven"—only four words. But what wealth of meaning in them, meaning we want our hearts to treasure each time we pray.

Prayer: Heavenly Father, thank you for making me your child through faith in Jesus. Help me come to you confidently with all my needs. Amen.

The Lord's Prayer

"Hallowed be your name."

We do all kinds of things with names. Names may mean a little or a lot to us, depending on the person they represent. They are treated with respect or repugnance, depending on what the person has or has not done for us. They are long remembered or soon forgotten, depending on what the person means to us. Names come and names go, but none is like the name of God. His name is above all names, as our use of his name should reflect.

May your word be kept holy

How do we get from "hallowed be your name" to "may your Word be kept holy"? We start by looking at what a name is. Let's use the name Abraham Lincoln as an example. Mention his name and we think of the man who was our country's 16th president, of words he spoke (such as the Gettysburg Address), of what he did to preserve our country, of how he stood firm in hard times of conflict. His name represents all we know about him—what he was and said and did: his entire person and personality.

Even more so when we pray about God's name in the First Petition. God's name is all that we know about him and his person, his words and his works. And that brings us to God's Word. For it is only in his Word that God shows us his name. On the sacred pages of

Scripture, he tells us *who* he is: triune God, Father, Son, and Holy Spirit. In the same book, he tells us *what* he is: almighty, all-knowing, all-present, eternal, merciful, loving. There too he tells us what he has said—how at Sinai he thundered his Law to show us what we are and at Calvary whispered his gospel to show us what he had done about our condition. Speak of God's name and we are at the same time speaking about his Word.

I've never seen pure gold, but they tell me it's 24 carat. There is no such thing as 26-carat gold. You can't add anything to pure gold to make it any purer. You can, however, dilute it into 18 or 14 carat by mixing in other metals. So God's name is "certainly holy by itself." God is holy; his person is holy; his works are holy; his Word is holy. No more than we can beef up 24-carat gold can we make his holy name *more* holy. To pray that God's name be hallowed is not asking that his word be made holy but rather that it be kept that way.

May we keep your word holy by true teaching and living

God's Word is holy by itself, and he could keep it so. He has, however, put it into our shaky hands—and that's where the need for this petition enters in. When we pray "hallowed be your name," we're asking God to help us *keep* it holy through true teaching and true living. Our concern to keep his Word unpolluted should make the environmentalist's concern for earth's resources tiny by comparison. When people twist the Word to make it say what they want, tone down the Word to make it sound sweeter, trim out the Word to make it more modern, they are doing no one a favor. They pollute God's Word with disastrous results for themselves, those around them, and all who hear them.

Similarly, when people mouth the Word but don't model it in their lives, God's name is debased. When unbelievers fail to see kindness in our homes, uprightness in our dealings, joy in our hearts, confidence in our hours of death, why should they want to become like us or honor God's name with us? Luther's words are right on: "Keep us from doing this, dear Father in heaven!"

"Hallowed be your name"—let those words be my *prayer for divine forgiveness* for the many times my feet have dragged mud over his Word and my life has been but a flickering match tip in sin's darkness. "Hallowed be your name"—let those words be my *prayer of pledge* with which I bind myself to study his Word more fully, so that I can speak it more clearly. "Hallowed be your name"—let those words be my *prayer for divine help* to speak up and not be silent in this anti-Christian society and to put the trump on my words with my actions, even when those actions are out of step with the world's ways. Again Luther's words hit the mark: "Help us to do this, dear Father in heaven!"

Jesus, who was God's name in person, could say: "I am the Light of the Word. Look at me and know God." Now we who bear his name pray that he help us let our lights shine, so that others can see what he is and what he can do for them.

Prayer: Heavenly Father, help us keep your name holy by true preaching and true living. Amen.

The Lord's Prayer

"Your kingdom come."

In my day it was called geography—that class in which we had to memorize the names of countries and their capitals. We also learned something about the main characteristics and commodities of each country. Over the years I've forgotten much of what I learned in those classes. I'm also glad that I'm no longer in geography class, or whatever they call it today, with so many countries changing or choosing new names. When it comes to God's country, or as our petition calls it, his kingdom, there has been no change. Its makeup is still the same and so are its characteristics.

A prayer for ourselves

I'm a citizen of the United States because I was born here. Two of our children were, for a time, also citizens of Canada because they were born there. Entry into God's kingdom, however, does not depend on place of birth. His kingdom is not a land contained by the Atlantic and Pacific Oceans, comprised of a certain number of states, composed of all who live therein. God's kingdom is made up of people, very special people, people living across the globe.

Who might they be? Jesus, the loving ruler of this kingdom, tells us. At the beginning of his ministry, he preached: "The kingdom of God is near. Repent and believe the good news!" (Mark 1:15). Near the end of his ministry, he promised the dying thief who prayed for remembrance in the kingdom, "Today you will be with me in paradise" (Luke 23:43). God's kingdom is an invisible one, made up of all who trust in Jesus as the only Savior from sin. Entrance into this kingdom of grace comes not by birth but rebirth; not through parents who give breath but the Spirit who works faith. It comes only by the power of the gospel—counting in its numbers the smallest baby carried to the cross of Christ by Baptism, as well as the oldest grandparent kept confident to the end in the blood of Christ by the Word. "My kingdom is not of this world," Jesus once told Pilate (John 18:36). It's a heavenly one, a kingdom of grace, because it's made up of all in whom his Spirit works faith through the means of grace, the gospel in Word and sacrament.

And I'm part of it! "Your kingdom come" is my *prayer of appreciation,* my looking heavenward with grateful eyes to the one whose grace has plucked me out of Satan's kingdom of darkness. It's also my *prayer for assistance,* showing clearly my realization that faith continues, only as it comes, by the working of the Spirit. And it's my *prayer of assurance,* expressing my confidence that he who, by creating faith, has brought me into Christ's wonderful kingdom will also keep me in faith until I reach its fullness in heaven.

A prayer for others

It's not selfish in this petition to pray for ourselves before we pray for others. Those outside of God's kingdom have no concern that others be in it. Those within his kingdom can only pray that others join them. So this petition is a *prayer for conversion:* "Your kingdom come," we pray every time a baby is carried to our church's baptismal font. "Your kingdom come," we pray with each effort to teach the Word to our family or reach out to our neighbor with it. "Your kingdom come," we pray as we serve in whatever way we ourselves can where we are and also send missionaries to different cities and foreign lands. "Send your Holy Spirit to work with your powerful gospel, not only in our hearts but in the hearts of many others," is our ongoing prayer.

With the prayer for conversion of others, we couple the *prayer for commitment by ourselves*. Visiting a congregation recently, I asked some of the members, "What do you like about your church?" "Missions," they replied. When I probed further, they answered: "We don't talk missions. We do missions." We cannot pray this petition and show apathy, a "you can take it or leave it" approach to missions. We cannot pray this petition and show sympathy, a "it's good to do mission work, but let others do it" approach. This prayer calls for energy, a "it's my work and I'm going to do it" approach. It's God kingdom, and it comes of itself without our prayers, in spite of the base efforts of the devil to stop it. But God has graciously made us his partners in getting the Word out—the Word through which he makes his kingdom come.

So what if we forget those other countries about which they try to teach us. Those countries won't be around forever. God's kingdom, however, will. Our prayer is that he keep us in his kingdom and use us to help bring others to it.

Prayer: Heavenly Father, may your kingdom come to me and to many others. Amen.

The Lord's Prayer

"Your will be done on earth as in heaven."

Have you made out your will yet? When I started traveling for world missions, my wife and I went to a lawyer and had our will drawn up. In it we put down what we wanted done with our possessions, including our most precious possessions, our small children. Periodically we update that will as the circumstances of our lives change. There it is for others to someday carry out.

God has a will. There are things he wants. On the pages of the Bible, he has written them down. With his will no updating is ever necessary, because he never changes his mind. Though some act as if God has no will or contest it constantly, it will surely be carried out.

What God wants

People have so many strange ideas about what God wants. They prattle and preach about this and that, forgetting that what God wants he has written down. Do we need a refresher? Listen to Jesus: "My Father's will is that everyone who looks to the Son and believes in him shall have eternal life" (John 6:40). Listen to Paul as he amplifies this thought: "[God] wants all men to be saved and to come to a knowledge of the truth" (1 Timothy 2:3,4). What God wants for you and me and for everyone is that they believe in Jesus and be saved eternally.

There's more. "It is God's will that you should be sanctified," Paul reminded the Christians at Thessalonica (1 Thessalonians 4:3). God wants those who belong to his family to live like family members. He wants them, as his willing children, to do what he wants and to avoid what he does not want. We can understand this, for don't we expect the same in our earthly families?

What the almighty God wants, he makes happen. Unlike some football game with opposing teams seesawing across the field and not winning until the final whistle, God is in control. Though we can't always see it, his power works in the hearts and lives of those he chooses. With this Third Petition, we are not implying that we can make his holy, saving will happen. We're praying that he work it among us also.

What others want

Not everyone wants what God wants. In case we haven't noticed lately, three major enemies have lined up in opposition to his will. There's the devil. His defeat has already occurred, but he's not sulking in hell, licking his wounds. With the bitter sting of defeat in his heart, he rages all the more fiercely, especially against God's children. Those already doing his devilish will need sporadic attention; those doing God's will need his special attacks. There's the world with whom the devil partners. Like those d-Con packages we set out in our homes to eliminate mice, so the world, in every season of life, strews its tasty morsels before us to thin out and even kill off our faith. And there's the enemy we can never get away from, for we carry it inside of us wherever we go. Like some gasoline can, our sinful nature sits there ready to explode at the slightest flame.

Oh yes, we've noticed these three enemies. They've done more than attack us. They've taken big chunks out of us and left us bleeding. By ourselves we can't stop them, and if unstopped they will kill us. That's why we pray this petition to our almighty, loving Father in heaven.

What we want

So what are we asking with this petition? First, we pray for *God's saving power*. With his cross on Calvary, he put Satan down for the count, the world in its place, and the padlock on our sinful hearts. God did not exhaust his saving power on Calvary, but uses it each day to reinforce his mighty victory. If only we could see how often God keeps away the vicious attacks of the devil, the world, and our flesh, we would ask more fervently with this petition that he continue to do so.

Second, we pray for *God's strengthening power*. Only he can bulk up the muscles of faith and build up stamina for Christian living. If only we would remember how he does this, we would turn more frequently to his Word. The gospel is his power unto salvation, not only bringing us to faith but keeping us in faith in Jesus. The gospel is his power, making his will our will and moving us to follow that will more in our lives. When we pray this petition, we are also promising to turn to that gospel for his power.

Someday we'll join the saints and angels in doing God's will perfectly in heaven. Until that time comes, we need to pray "your will be done on earth as in heaven."

Prayer: Lord, thank you for bringing us to faith in Jesus. Keep that faith in us and in our lives in spite of the attacks of the devil, the world, and our flesh. Amen.

The Lord's Prayer

"Give us today our daily bread."

Only one in seven! That's right—only one of the seven petitions, or requests, in the Lord's Prayer deals with bodily needs. What a reminder for us to get our values straight when we pray. Don't think that the Lord is not concerned about taking care of our physical needs and that we should never pray about them. If such were the case, he would not have included a petition about daily bread in his prayer. But he has, and we use the Fourth Petition with gratitude and confidence.

Our daily bread

For us in the West it's bread; in Latin America its tortillas; in the Far East its rice—but the meaning is the same. "Bread" means that which we need to live. "Daily," its original meaning indicating what we need for the moment, reinforces the thought. In explaining "daily bread," Luther included the things we need, the circumstances we need, and the people we need in order to live. "Give me neither poverty nor riches, but give me only my daily bread," wise Solomon prayed (Proverbs 30:8), and we would do well to follow his lead.

Yet so often we turn the word *bread* into *cake*, and when God gives "cake," we even ask for thicker frosting. Because God in his goodness grants extras, we slowly but surely confuse wants with needs. Bread becomes fancy food. House becomes not just a roof over our heads but one finer than our neighbor's. Family becomes one that is superior to anyone else's. Job and income become one that surpasses that of my relatives'. The more our gracious God gives, the more we want. And when he doesn't give us "cake," we pout and even point an accusing finger at him. "Daily bread," Jesus said, "that which we need in order to live."

Today

"Today," Jesus teaches us to pray, reminding us that asking for bread should be not sporadic but a daily practice. That word *today* serves also as an antidote against worry. Yesterday is past and cannot be changed. Why lug its troubles along, like so much mold to taint the taste of today's bread? Tomorrow is farther than we can see, much less control. Why allow its supposed troubles, like some half-baked dough, to lie in our stomachs, spoiling our appetite for today's bread. Certainly the Lord, who cares for us daily, expects us to plan and perspire. But his word *today* rules out a brow furrowed with anxiety and a heart feverish with worry. "Your heavenly Father knows that you need them," Jesus promised, referring to our daily bread and reassuring us of its coming (Matthew 6:32).

Do I hear you saying, "That's easier said than done?" Do you know what worries I have on my plate? What about my retirement investments and the cost of medicare rising? What about my job just hanging by a string, with the scissors ready to snip? What about the braces my child needs on his teeth or those cells running haywire in my body? What about not finding a mate or having no friends? Yes, what about??? Jesus has the answer. "Today" he taught us to pray, leaving yesterday and tomorrow in our loving Father's hands.

Only he can forgive and correct yesterday's failures, and only he can supply tomorrow's needs.

Give

Does the word *give* suggest something we aren't so ready to hear? We'd rather push back in our La-Z-Boy recliners and pronounce: "I have planned. I have perspired. I have profited." Or to put it another way, "I have earned my daily bread." Other times we look around and then grumble, "Lord, I deserve more or at least as much as you've given that fellow next door." Again it's talk about earning or deserving. When Jesus said "give," he's speaking to us of a *prayer of humility*. With this word he reminds us to stand, not toe-to-toe, eyeball-to-eyeball with God, but down in the dust as a beggar before him. Daily bread is not my paycheck; it's God's gift to me.

"Give" is also a *prayer of thanksgiving*. God expects his children to stand taller than the unbelieving people and the ungrateful beasts in this world, who grab and gulp their daily bread, giving no thought to the gracious hand behind it. God's children thank the giver before using the gift. When we pray "give" in regards to daily bread, we are reminded to bow our heads in daily thanksgiving and bend our lives for daily "thanksliving."

Only one petition in seven, but no less important. Where would we be without God giving us today our daily bread?

Prayer: Giver of all, help me with lips and life to thank you for my daily bread. Amen.

The Lord's Prayer

"Forgive us our sins, as we forgive those who sin against us."

Which is the greatest petition in the Lord's Prayer? Can there be any doubt? It has to be the Fifth Petition, with its words about forgiveness of sins. Unless we pray this petition, we cannot pray any of the others. We must have forgiveness before we can carry anything to God in prayer. Also, once we have experienced divine forgiveness, we extend it to others.

Our greatest need

What a motivator need is. Before we seek a doctor's help, we have to feel our sickness. Before we say "help me" to anyone about anything, need has to press our nose to the floor. So also with our prayer to God for his forgiveness. Can it be that at times we slide over the words of this petition or speak them listlessly because we don't feel our pressing need?

Not King David. He tried to anesthetize his conscience and cover his sins of adultery and murder. But the more he tried, the more he felt God's heavy hand. Only when he confessed "Against you, you only, have I sinned and done what is evil in your sight," could he revel in the joy of God's salvation (Psalm 51:4). Not Simon Peter. He warmed his hands and singed his soul that Thursday night around the campfire in the high priest's courtyard. His tears came, but not because his blustery denial and bold-faced lying felt light as a feather to him. Not the apostle Paul either. "Chief of sinners" he kept on labeling himself, even as he marveled at God's grace that would turn a persecutor into a preacher.

"Not like them," are we thinking? "My sins are not so great, my need for forgiveness not so heavy," are we theorizing? Watch out! The cataracts sin grows over our eyes and the macular degeneration it causes in our vision blur our view of sin. When God said "Be holy because I, the LORD your God, am holy," he wasn't suggesting that he might be satisfied with something less than one hundred percent from us (Leviticus 19:2). When his apostle said "Everyone who sins breaks the law," he wasn't setting up some kind of sin-o-meter with which to measure the seriousness of our sins (1 John 3:4). In God's eyes, every thought, word, or deed that misses the mark of his commandments is not just a debt that burdens but one that breaks the sinner's back. When we pray this petition, and we need to do so daily, we are asking God *to awaken our conscience to our many sins* and our pressing need for daily forgiveness.

Our greatest gift

On Calvary's cross God did what the burdened sinner could not do. He cleared our account by drawing a crimson line through our debt. "The blood of Jesus, his Son, purifies us from all sin," the apostle assures us (1 John 1:7). Don't think it was easy for God to forgive our sins. It cost him the best he had, his eternal Son, and it cost that Son the best he had, his life. Don't think either that God *had* to prepare forgiveness for us. Not what was in us but what was in him prompted that forgiveness. His love drove him, a love that can only be divine. His grace reaches for us, a grace that offers sinners what they don't deserve.

At Calvary, God prepared full forgiveness for our every sin. When we pray this petition, we are asking him to *assure our hearts of this great treasure.* How can we close our eyes in peace at night without using this petition for one more glance at Calvary's cross?

Our greatest response

Someone once wrote, "To repay good with evil is devil-like. To repay evil with evil is beastlike. To repay good with good is manlike. To repay evil with good is Godlike." How true! When we pray "as we forgive those who sin against us," we are *asking God for his assistance* to make us more like him. We're not cutting a deal with him in which he promises to forgive us because we forgive those around us. We're stating a blessed fact. Because he has forgiven our many sins, we, as a result, offer the same forgiveness for the few sins our neighbor commits against us. Just as we naturally breathe if we are physically alive, so we forgive if we are spiritually alive in Christ.

Hard to do? Of course. Impossible to do? Not according to this Fifth Petition. When God pours his great forgiveness into our reaching, repentant hands, he also powers them to pass that same gift on to others.

Prayer: Heavenly Father, make us more like you so that we forgive others as you have forgiven us. For Jesus' sake. Amen.

The Lord's Prayer

"Lead us not into temptation."

"Dear Abby," the letter went, "how come all the people we see doing exercises on those tapes are slim and trim?" Her answer, "Because it takes exercise to get into and stay in shape." In the Sixth Petition, our Lord teaches us to pray about exercise, about what it takes for us to get into and stay spiritually in shape.

What we pray God to do

Temptation is actually a neutral word. In the original it means "testing," some proving or probing, if you will. Scripture uses this word in two different ways. When it speaks of God tempting, it refers to his testing a believer with the view of strengthening faith. He once did this by asking Abraham to sacrifice Isaac. He did it also to Paul by giving him a physical ailment and then refusing to remove it. When Scripture speaks of the devil, world, and flesh tempting, the opposite is true. Always when this unholy trio approaches, it's to damage and destroy faith. That's what happened with Adam and Eve in the Garden of Eden and with Judas in the Garden of Gethsemane. With his temptations, God wants to root faith deeper in his Word, while the devil's intentions are to rip those roots out of that nourishing soil.

With this petition, are we asking God to stop testing our faith? Hardly! How flabby faith's muscles would become if he didn't put them through some calisthenics. Rather, we're asking God to do something about those nasty efforts of the devil, the world, and our flesh. Though temptations to evil *never* come from our holy, loving Father, he is more than capable of stopping them or giving us the ability to conquer them when they do attack.

Do we need this petition when we ask *God to use his strength in our behalf?* Not if we follow the world's wisdom that says, "The only way to get rid of temptation is to give in to it." If we are at all serious about faith and Christian living, if we've learned the lesson that regardless where we move, temptation finds our forwarding address, if we've discovered that temptations get not fewer but different as we grow older, then we know how much we need to ask our Father in heaven for those two S's—that he either stop temptation or strengthen us to win over them.

What we promise ourselves to do

This petition is also our way of *announcing what we will do.* "Don't worry, Dad," the little boy says as he climbs up the tree, "I won't fall." And you know what's going to happen before you get there to catch him. "If you think you are standing firm, be careful that you don't fall!" Paul warned (1 Corinthians 10:12). Noah squeezing grapes into wine, David looking at a lovely woman in her bath, Judas fingering slippery coins in his purse would have done well to heed Paul's advice. So do we. The first step to fighting temptation is remembering our weakness.

The second step is staying out of temptation's way. Admittedly that's difficult because temptation is all around us. Temptations constantly walk down our street, but we don't have to open the door and invite them in. Playing around with temptation is like trying to run down a mountainside. There comes a time when your legs get away from you and you can no longer stop.

The third step is knowing where to find strength. "God is faithful; he will not let you be tempted beyond what you can bear. But when you are tempted, he will also provide a way out so that you can stand up under it," Paul promised (1 Corinthians 10:13). When the bully of temptation blocks our path and threatens to bloody our nose, we don't foolishly take it on by ourselves. Nor do we stand there shaking in fear until it demolishes us. We get our bigger brother. Jesus knows what to do to overcome the evil one. In the wilderness he sent the devil packing with the words "it is written." "Take . . . the sword of the Spirit, which is the word of God," he advises us (Ephesians 6:17).

And still we fall. The devil wins, the world triumphs, our flesh yields. Then what? Then it's time to remember the fifth rule in fighting temptation and look to Jesus for pardon. It's time to see the love in his eyes that says, "I'm disappointed, but I still love you." It's time to see the wounds in his hands that say, "I stretched these out in bitter payment for those very sins, and now I stretch them out in genuine welcome to you." It's time to hear his soft, yet wondrously sweet voice assuring, "Arise, go in peace, your sins are forgiven."

Then all the more, we'll promise to do all we can to keep fit for the fight against temptation. God, help us! Amen.

The Lord's Prayer

"But deliver us from evil."

Did you ever try ringing a church bell? What a lesson in prayer this can be. Back in the parish I served, we had three bells that the eighth-grade boys used to ring before our Friday children's service. They quickly learned that you didn't just pull the rope once, not even just two or three times. To get those bells sweetly ringing in the steeple took vigorous, repeated rope pulling. Just imagine what might happen if we pulled and pulled on the bell rope of prayer with this Seventh Petition.

Evil—what is it?

It's not that we don't know what evil is. It's rather that there's so much of it around us that we hardly know where to start. Luther summarizes them as evils that "threaten body and soul, property and reputation." For the body there are lungs that can't breathe and kidneys that fail, cells that grow wild and lymph glands that spread cancer. There are bodies that go hungry and bodies that grow old. There are accidents, diseases, and death. For property there's the moth of inflation, the rust of recession, the mold of unemployment, the doors we must lock on our homes and cars, the smoke alarms and fire stations so often necessary, the lack of rain and then again too much of it. For our reputation there's deceitful lies, gossip and slander, betrayal of confidences or sins and the like, all dredged up from the swamp of hell by the greatest liar of all, the devil.

Let's not forget the greatest evil of all, that which threatens the soul. There's indifference to the soul's needs leading to spiritual death by slow starvation. Trusting in one's own works self-righteously pushing the Savior out of the picture. Worldliness misdirecting the soul fatally into the backwaters of possession and pleasure. False teachings deluding the soul's taste buds with their poison. Ill will and quarrels, jealousies and hatred causing the soul to shed bitter tears.

And behind all this evil? Not God. Evil is not his creation but sin's child. The devil brought sin, and sin brought evil—all those untold evils of body and soul, property and reputation. Note carefully, fellow believers, *sin* is behind all evil, not *your* sin is behind all evil. In the hospital room, the counseling chamber, and the funeral home Christians sometimes lament, "God must be punishing me for my sins." "There is now no condemnation for those who are in Christ Jesus," Paul reminds us emphatically in Romans 8:1. Read "condemnation" as "punishment," and you'll understand what he's saying. God has already punished all our sins in Christ. For the penitent sinner who stands in the shadow of Christ's cross, the evils in this world are not punishment but the fall-out, the ashes that still cling to our lives.

Deliverance—where do we get it?

This petition is not a prayer of hopelessness but a prayer of *certainty and confidence*. We have a Father who can and will deliver us from all evil. "The Lord knows how to rescue godly men from trials," Peter affirmed (2 Peter 2:9). "Call upon me in the day of trouble; I will deliver you," our Father himself promised (Psalm 50:15). From sin, the greatest evil, he has already delivered us. Through the work of his Son, Jesus, he has struck cleanly off our wrists the handcuffs of sin; chopped completely through the chain of guilt, by which Satan was reeling us into hell; clanked tightly shut the door of hell, yawning wide open before us. He has freed us forever from sin's curse. He also hears and answers when we carry our daily sins of weakness to him and beg for deliverance.

The other evils of body and soul, property and reputation we also carry confidently to him in this petition. When we do, we add, "Your will be done." We may have our own ideas and even want to dictate the answers, but he knows much better than we do what form our deliverance should take for our greatest good. Sometimes he ends the storm and sends the rainbow almost immediately. Other times he uses continued troubles to teach us about our own weakness and his great strength and to develop patient hope, like some tough callous on faith's hands.

With this last petition, our Lord teaches us a second lesson. He intends it to be our prayer of *anticipation*. Can we even faintly imagine what the final deliverance in heaven will be like? Where there'll be no more pain or sorrow or any such thing. Where God will wipe away all tears from our eyes. Where we'll no longer need to pray "deliver us from evil," because it will all be gone.

But while we're still here on earth, we need this prayer daily. Just imagine what could happen if all God's children pulled vigorously on the bell rope of this prayer.

Prayer: Dear Jesus, help me bear up under the troubles of this world, and take me to be free from evil someday in heaven. Amen.

The Lord's Prayer

"For the kingdom, the power, and the glory are yours now and forever. Amen."

Coming through Chicago, I drove over a piece of debris on the tollway. Fortunately the punctured tire held up until I reached the outskirts, where I stopped to change it. Later as I drove on, I thought about prayer. Is prayer the spare tire in the trunk of life? Something we don't think much about until our life has a puncture? And then when we use it, something we shouldn't expect too much of, because its doughnut size is good only for limited mileage?

That's not how Jesus wants us to use the prayer he taught us. This he impresses on us with its concluding words.

A confident conclusion

We've asked tremendously great things of our Father in this prayer. Can he come through with what we've asked? Yes, the conclusion tells us, pointing not to us but to him. "For" it says. Read this word in your mind's eye as "because." We can ask confidently because the kingdom is his. To the unbelieving world, his kingdom means power—such as the power Pharaoh felt when the Red Sea waters washed over his chariots. For us, as believers, kingdom refers more to God's grace. It points us to a loving God whose grace in Christ Jesus has made us his dear children. We can enter his throne room confidently anytime and ask about those really important things—such as keeping his Word holy with our preaching and living and keeping us in and bringing others into his kingdom. When we pray "yours is the kingdom," it's especially his grace that makes us confident.

"Because yours is the power," we continue. A king without power is like a car without an engine—nice looking, but going nowhere. Not our Father in heaven. Joshua prayed—and the sun stood still. Elijah prayed—and the drought of three years and six months ended. The disciples prayed—and the storm stopped. Paul and Silas prayed—and the earthquake sprung the cell doors of the jail. The one to whom we pray has the power to raise the dead and to pronounce forgiveness to the paralyzed. He has power to make Baptism's water cleanse our souls and to couple his very body and blood with the bread and wine for the communicant. Hesitate to come to him? Let his power hurry us to his throne with confidence.

"Because yours is the glory," we also pray. One of a man's great glories is that he's known for keeping his word. How much more so with our Father. "I will deliver you, and you will honor [glorify] me," he tells us (Psalm 50:15). In the Lord's Prayer, we give him glory simply by asking him. We also ask each petition with his glory in mind. And finally, we trust his answers to result in glory for him. To such a Father, we come with confidence. The kingdom and the power and the glory were his in eternity, are now, and ever shall be.

A confident word

"Amen," we pray, not as a signal that prayer is over but as a sure sign of our confidence. This sweet word has found its way into almost all of the languages of the world. It's one of the first prayer words we learned as infants. "Amen" means certainly, truly, surely. It's not a question mark but an exclamation point. With this word we aren't questioning, "Will you, Lord?" We're expressing the confidence, "You will, Lord!" When we pray "Amen," we shut the door to unbelief and doubt. We are telling our Father that we believe he has heard and will answer all that we have asked for in this prayer. How can it be otherwise? Our Father has commanded us to pray. Our Savior has taught us this prayer and made it possible for us to pray it by making us God's children. He even sends his Holy Spirit to help us when we pray (Romans 8:26).

"The Amen People" Luther once labeled believers. When things go wrong and we don't get what we want or as soon as we want it, it can be hard to be "Amen People." Then it's time again to turn to Jesus, God's great Amen, the one in whom he has fulfilled all his promises. In Jesus we receive pardon for the past, power in the present, and promise of the future. Our loving heavenly Father said "amen" first in him. Now we can say it too.

Prayer: Father in heaven, we believe that because of Jesus you hear us when we pray and that you will answer our prayers in the way best for us. Amen.

The Sacrament of Holy Baptism

The Institution of Baptism

First: What is Baptism?

Baptism is not just plain water, but it is water used by God's command and connected with God's Word.

What is that word of God?

Christ our Lord says in the last chapter of Matthew, "Go and make disciples of all nations, baptizing them in the name of the Father and of the Son and of the Holy Spirit."

The Blessings of Baptism

Second: What does Baptism do for us?

Baptism works forgiveness of sins, delivers from death and the devil, and gives eternal salvation to all who believe this, as the words and promises of God declare.

What are these words and promises of God?

Christ our Lord says in the last chapter of Mark, "Whoever believes and is baptized will be saved, but whoever does not believe will be condemned."

The Power of Baptism

Third: How can water do such great things?

It is certainly not the water that does such things, but God's Word which is in and with the water and faith which trusts this Word used with the water.

For without God's Word the water is just plain water and not Baptism. But with this Word it is Baptism, that is, a gracious water of life and a washing of rebirth by the Holy Spirit.

Where is this written?

Saint Paul says in Titus, Chapter 3, "[God] saved us through the washing of rebirth and renewal by the Holy Spirit, whom he poured out on us generously through Jesus Christ our Savior, so that, having been justified by his grace, we might become heirs having the hope of eternal life. This is a trustworthy saying."

The Meaning of Baptism for Our Daily Life

Fourth: What does baptizing with water mean?

Baptism means that the old Adam in us should be drowned by daily contrition and repentance, and that all its evil deeds and desires be put to death. It also means that a new person should daily arise to live before God in righteousness and purity forever.

Where is this written?

Saint Paul says in Romans, chapter 6, "We were . . . buried with [Christ] through baptism into death in order that, just as Christ was raised from the dead through the glory of the Father, we too may live a new life."

Holy Baptism

"Baptism is not just plain water, but it is water used by God's command and connected with God's Word."

He had watched me sprinkling drops of water on his baby sister's head at the baptismal font. With the curiosity of a four-year-old, he asked, "Why did you wet her head?" When I explained, "To make Susie Jesus' own child," he came right back with the logic of a four-year-old, "Why didn't you use more water?" Water is all most people see when it comes to Baptism. But there's more, so much more, behind the water in this sacrament.

Water connected with God's Word

God commanded us to baptize. In the last chapter of Matthew, Christ our Lord said, "Go and make disciples of all nations, baptizing them in the name of the Father and of the Son and of the Holy Spirit." In this command are his answers to our questions about Baptism.

What does it mean to *baptize?* The word itself means "to apply water." Sometimes the Bible uses the term *baptize* for religious washing, other times for cleansing hands, dishes, or even household furnishings. Depending on the size of the object and the availability of water, the word could mean "to pour, wash, sprinkle" or "to immerse." Since the Lord Jesus did not limit the word *baptize* to a particular way of application, we too leave it open. And yes, I could have used a bucket full of water on little Susie, but sprinkling was far more convenient.

Who is to be baptized? "All nations," Jesus commanded. Just as all are counted in a nation's census, so Jesus intended Baptism for all, including infants. We might even say Baptism is especially for babies. They face sin's wage along with the rest of us, but, unlike us, have no other way of receiving eternal life except through Baptism. Their faith, just as ours, is a miraculous gift of the Spirit and depends not on the ability to know facts or make confession. So, yes, little Susie belonged at that baptismal font.

Who does the baptizing? To this day Jesus places the authority to open heaven's door in the hands of his disciples, the believers. In cases of emergency, any believer may and will use Baptism for the needy soul before him. Under normal circumstances believers give that authority to their pastors, so that all things might be done decently and orderly. Or as Luther once put it, so we don't drown the little ones by all trying to do the baptizing. That's why I was at that baptismal font with little Susie, not only as the hand and mouth of Jesus but also as the hand and mouth of the believers in the congregation.

Water used by God's command

What can water do for us in Baptism? Just plain water has no more power than the water we put into our soup pots or heat to make our coffee. Even if a ton of water were poured over us, it would do us no good. By connecting something so commonplace with Baptism, the Lord was lifting our attention from the element to the essential, from the water to his Word. In his Word is the power. And what a powerful Word has he connected with Baptism. "Make disciples of all nations," he commanded, "baptizing them in the name of the Father and of the Son and of the Holy Spirit." "In" expresses close connection and could also be translated "into." "Name" is the gospel summed up in one word. Simply put, *to be baptized into his name* is to be brought into a blessed relationship with the triune God in which, as a member of his family, we enjoy all his blessings.

That's what was happening with little Susie. The triune God himself came to her in that water and promised: "I am your Father, and I now make you my child to live with me forever. And though you were born in sin to be the devil's child, I gave you my own Son. He died for you and washed away your sin. And I gave you my Holy Spirit. He opens your heart to trust Jesus as your Savior and to love him dearly. "And I mean it," he continues, "I want your adoption into my family to stand forever." Though we can, through unbelief, become runaways of his family, his promise, made with us at our baptism, stands waiting for us.

Because for many of us Baptism came at an early date in life and lies somewhere in the past, we may not think of it often. What a mistake! Let our daily thought be not "I *was* baptized" but "I *am* baptized." Our Lord's baptismal promise of membership in his heavenly family is something for us to treasure every day.

Prayer: "My loving Father, there you took me
To be henceforth your child and heir.
My faithful Savior, there you let me
The fruit of all your sorrows share.
O Holy Spirit, comfort me
When threat'ning clouds around I see." Amen.

(CW 294:2)

Holy Baptism

"Baptism works forgiveness of sin, delivers from death and the devil, and gives eternal salvation to all who believe this, as the words and promises of God declare."

September 15—that's what it was for me. On that date, two weeks plus after my birth, something superimportant happened, bringing me a gift that lasts forever. What was September 15? The day of my baptism! Because the day of our baptism is so far in the past for most of us and before the time we started memories, we might have to rummage around for our baptismal certificates to verify the date. But it's worth looking up. Even more so it is worth remembering and celebrating on a daily basis.

His gracious work

There's "a working" going on at the baptismal font. The question is, who's doing it. Not the parents who carry their little one there. Not the pastor who cups the water in his hand. Not the tiny one cradled in its sponsor's arms. The real work is being done by a gracious God. So the words of our catechism tell us. Not we, but Baptism works, delivers, and gives. Just as little as a patient lying anaesthetized on the operating room table assists a doctor with surgery, do we work with the Lord in Baptism.

Baptism is God's work, something he does to us and for us—not for his own sake but for ours. He sees people who are born sinful and needing salvation. He sees people incapable of saving themselves and capable only of speeding onward, or should we say downward, in dead unbelief. And with his grace, he steps forward to that baptismal font to do what only he can do. Through the power of his promise connected with the water in that font, he puts the sign of his Son's cross, not just outwardly on our heads but inwardly on our hearts. With one simple act, he cracks open hearts dead in unbelief and creates faith in the Savior. Carried to that baptismal font as his enemies, we leave as his dear children and heirs of all he offers in Christ Jesus. A day to remember? Absolutely, because of what a gracious God does for us in Baptism.

Our great wealth

Notice that the words of the catechism speak not of the past but of the present. Baptism "works . . . delivers . . . gives," it says. The blessings God placed into the hand of faith that he created through our baptism are for our daily usage. Notice also that these blessings, described as "forgiveness of sins, deliverance from death and the devil, and eternal salvation" can be summed up with one word: *save.* That's what Peter said when comparing Baptism to the floodwaters that lifted up Noah's ark to safety. "Baptism . . . now *saves* you," he summarized (1 Peter 3:21).

When God worked faith in our hearts through Baptism, he at the same time dressed us for his family. Christ's robe of righteousness, woven with his death and resurrection, was draped over us and belted around us. Now when our Father looks at us, he no longer sees our sins, but the forgiveness prepared by his Son. With sin removed, death's sting is also gone. Like some lion, death still roars at us, but it has no claws of hell to rip our souls. Against its will, death even becomes our helper, ushering us into eternity above. And the devil, what can he really do to us? Yes, he sometimes still tricks us and trips us into sin, but the sign of the cross on our heart tells him plainly to whom we belong. "Hands off," the cross states clearly, "this one belongs to me." From the moment of our baptism on, we experience the peace the world cannot give, the joy of the redeemed of God, the security of his guidance and protection—all that goes with "eternal salvation," as we'll find out fully in heaven.

When the immigration officer at the Canadian border asked me about my citizenship, I didn't answer, "I was a citizen of the United States." My birth made me that and still makes me that. So when it comes to my heavenly citizenship, let's not answer "I *was* a citizen of heaven" but "I *am*." God's gracious working through Baptism did that for me and still does. When I wonder, then it's time to go back to his promise connected with the water on that special day. For me it was September 15. When was it for you?

Prayer: "My faithful God, you fail me never;
Your promise surely will endure.
Oh, cast me not away forever
If words and deeds become impure.
Have mercy when I come defiled;
Forgive, lift up, restore your child." Amen.

(CW 294:3)

Holy Baptism

"It is certainly not the water that does such things, but God's Word which is in and with the water and faith which trusts this Word used with the water. For without God's Word the water is just plain water and not Baptism. But with this Word it is Baptism, that is, a gracious water of life and a washing of rebirth by the Holy Spirit."

One of the joys connected with the pastoral ministry is being God's hand and the congregation's representative in performing Baptisms. As I sprinkle water on a sleeping infant's head or splash it more liberally on the head of an adult, I find myself thinking, "If only we could see what was happening." Never again would we take Baptism for granted or grumble about the time it added to a worship service. We'd want to crowd around the baptismal font, if we could, or at least sit on the edge of our pew in rapt attention. And we'd surely want to concentrate on the words being used. For those divine words connect rich blessings with Baptism's water and create the faith needed to receive them. Yes, if only we could see what was happening!

Conveying Christ's blessings

Have you noticed the stress Luther placed on God's Word in Holy Baptism? "It [Baptism] is water used by God's command and connected with God's Word," he began. "Baptism works forgiveness of sin, delivers from death and the devil, and gives eternal salvation to all who believe this, as the words and promises of God declare," he continued. In the section before us he reaffirms, "It is certainly not the water that does such things, but God's Word which is in and with the water."

What would Baptism be without God's Word connected with it? At worst a superstitious washing—like the heathen bathing in a certain river and receiving nothing, regardless of how often or long they splash. At best a superficial Christian ceremony in which parents are the actors, reverently giving a name to their child and dedicating him or her to the Lord. Of course, water is important. God connected it with Baptism. But water by itself is nothing and can do nothing. Just as the water of the Jordan by itself could not cleanse General Naaman of his leprous sores (2 Kings 5), or just as the bronze snake, lifted up in Israel's camp, could not by itself rescue those bitten by the poisonous snakes (Numbers 21), so the water in Baptism without God's promise could wash away no sin. God cleanses us "by the washing with water through the word," Paul summarized so emphatically (Ephesians 5:26). As the water hits the head, God's Word of promise penetrates to the heart, conveying all the blessings he has prepared for us in Christ.

If only we could see at that baptismal font how God's hand reaches down with his word of promise to connect the blessings of salvation with the water of Baptism.

Creating Christian faith

Another *hand* is needed in Baptism—the *hand of faith* to receive those blessings. Not only is the sinner born without that hand, he cannot create it for himself. "Flesh gives birth to flesh," Jesus said in John 3:6. Just as we inherit our genetic makeup from our parents, we also inherit our spiritual makeup. And that puts us outside of God's kingdom with no hope of ever getting in. Sin is not just something we do now and then in moments of weakness. *It is something we are by birth.* Our inherited nature is utterly infected and horribly corrupted, shot through and through with unbelief. No more than a dead plant can water itself and cause new life, can the human heart come to faith and embrace Christ's treasures. Only as we realize how handicapped the sinner is, will we appreciate the miracle God performs at the baptismal font.

"No one can enter the kingdom of God unless he is born of water and the Spirit," Jesus said (John 3:5). This side of eternity, we'll never grasp the mystery in those words, but the method is no secret. Through the washing of water with the Word, the Spirit creates faith's hand to receive Christ's blessings. We are brought to the baptismal font as *Satan's child,* destined for his hell. And we are brought away from that font as *God's own child,* designated for a never-ending life. At that font, our name is not only given on earth but much more so, written by God's grace in heaven. The miracle of faith is ours, worked by the Spirit through God's powerful Word. The clenched fist of unbelief is turned, by his working, into the hand of faith, carrying home Christ's blessings.

If only we could see what happens at the baptismal font, we'd want to look again and again at our own baptism in thankfulness for the blessings it brings us and the faith to receive them.

Prayer: Thank you, gracious Lord, for my baptism that assures me:

> "Be of good cheer, for God's own Son
> Forgives the sins that you have done.
> You're justified by Jesus' blood;
> Baptized, you are a child of God." Amen.

(CW 391:4)

Holy Baptism

"Baptism means that the old Adam in us should be drowned by daily contrition and repentance, and that all its evil deeds and desires be put to death. It also means that a new person should daily arise to live before God in righteousness and purity forever."

"I was baptized." Is that the end of it? Satan would like us to think so. He tries desperately to lull us into viewing our baptism as a pillow on which to fall lazily asleep. On the contrary! Baptism is a call to arms against the old Adam, a commitment to lifelong battle against our inherited sinful nature, that once drowned in Baptism, yet reemerges daily to war against us. So Luther reminds us, "A Christian life is nothing else than a daily Baptism, once begun and ever continued. For we must keep at it incessantly, always purging out whatever pertains to the old Adam, so that whatever belongs to the new man may come forth" (Tappert, *Book of Concord*, page 445).

A repeated battle with a reemerging foe

The child carried to Baptism is buried there. What else can be done with a child whose nature is totally corrupt and whose legacy is only sin and guilt. To live, that child must first die. And that's what happens in Baptism. Baptism doesn't make our sinful nature better; it drowns and buries it. All because of God's grace in Christ. On the cross, Christ bore the guilt and paid the penalty for all our sins, both the actual sins in our lives and the original sin with which we were born. When he died as our substitute, we died in him. Through Baptism our share in his death for sin was given to us. But just as Christ did not remain in the grave, neither do we. Just as the resurrection brought him new life, so does our Baptism. Totally clean, we are carried away from that baptismal font, totally alive in faith, with a new heart beating in tune with our gracious Father's will.

If only it would continue that way! But the old Adam, like some tough dandelion, keeps sticking its head up again and again in the lawn of daily life. So durable is our sinful nature, that, when drowned, it doesn't drop to the bottom of the sea but comes to the surface again and again—not only gasping for air, but trying to squeeze the Christian breath from the believer's lungs. The soul, cleansed by Christ at the baptismal font and committed to loving God above all things, becomes a soul torn and tempted by the same foe to the point that it joins Paul in agonizing, "What I do is not the good I want to do; no, the evil I do not want to do—this I keep on doing" (Romans 7:19). If we've looked honestly at our hearts lately, we know exactly what Paul was talking about—this repeated battle with a reemerging enemy.

A repentant rejoicing in the Redeemer's grace

Though we sin daily, just as before our baptism, there is one all-important difference. We may lose the battle, but not the war. The old Adam does not have the final word—our Savior does. Through Baptism he sends his Spirit to give us the power to rise from our sins, repent sincerely of them, and be reassured of Christ's forgiveness for them. The new man we are in Christ not only tastes the bitter tears of repentance but also the sweet forgiveness already promised in Baptism. Like the prodigal son, we find the Father waiting for us when we come to our senses. At our baptism he promised to wrap us again and again in his arms, while the angels in heaven rejoice, and the old Adam is left to die among the swine. Nor does he ever break his promise, as we discover each time we return home.

But the old Adam keeps punching us, pummeling our kidneys, pushing us into the ropes of life. To disable him, we need to enable the new man. The child of God that we were made in Baptism is not to remain some 90-pound weakling whom our sinful nature can push around at will. Our Father doesn't want us to drag ourselves wearily to him each night, as some prodigal undernourished by the lean rations of the swine. He wants us to drink deeply of his life-giving Word and to grow strong through his Holy Supper. He wants us to arm ourselves with the sword of the Spirit that is always sharp, if we but swing it against our enemy. He wants us to pull the robe of Christ's righteousness more tightly around us, so that we stand bravely against our foe and boldly before our God.

My grandmother, when she moved in with us, put her framed baptismal certificate on the bedroom wall opposite her bed. Each morning she could look at it and be reassured that she was God's child, who could draw on his strength for the battle of the day before her. Each night she could look at it again and be reassured that she was God's child, who was forgiven by his grace for the lost battles of the day. For us too Baptism is divine assurance that we will win the war.

Prayer: "Destroy in me the lust of sin;
From all impureness make me clean.
Oh, grant me pow'r and strength, my God,
To strive against my flesh and blood." Amen.

(CW 471:2)

The Sacrament of Holy Communion

The Institution of Holy Communion

First: What is the Sacrament of Holy Communion?

It is the true body and blood of our Lord Jesus Christ under the bread and wine, instituted by Christ for us Christians to eat and to drink.

Where is this written?

The holy evangelists Matthew, Mark, Luke, and the apostle Paul tell us: Our Lord Jesus Christ, on the night he was betrayed, took bread; and when he had given thanks, he broke it and gave it to his disciples, saying, "Take and eat; this is my body, which is given for you. Do this in remembrance of me."

Then he took the cup, gave thanks, and gave it to them, saying, "Drink from it, all of you; this is my blood of the new covenant, which is poured out for you for the forgiveness of sins. Do this, whenever you drink it, in remembrance of me."

The Blessings of Holy Communion

Second: What blessing do we receive through this eating and drinking?

That is shown us by these words: "Given" and "poured out for you for the forgiveness of sins."

Through these words we receive forgiveness of sins, life, and salvation in this sacrament.

For where there is forgiveness of sins, there is also life and salvation.

The Power of Holy Communion

Third: How can eating and drinking do such great things?

It is certainly not the eating and drinking that does such things, but the words "Given" and "poured out for you for the forgiveness of sins."

These words are the main thing in this sacrament, along with the eating and drinking. And whoever believes these words has what they plainly say, the forgiveness of sins.

The Reception of Holy Communion

Fourth: Who, then, is properly prepared to receive this sacrament?

Fasting and other outward preparations may serve a good purpose, but he is properly prepared who believes these words: "Given" and "poured out for you for the forgiveness of sins."

But whoever does not believe these words or doubts them is not prepared, because the words "for you" require nothing but hearts that believe.

Holy Communion

"It is the true body and blood of our Lord Jesus Christ under the bread and wine, instituted by Christ for us Christians to eat and to drink."

She was crying. As she stood there in the row of communicants, Grandma Rebase was crying. The Russians had closed most of the churches in her native Estonia and even if she had been able to attend one, her life would have been in danger. For she was a high school teacher and as such was not allowed to pollute minds with religion. When she reached the age of 65, the authorities allowed her to emigrate to Canada to join her daughter. She also joined our little mission congregation in Sault Ste. Marie. There at Our Saviour's, she was privileged to receive the Lord's body and blood again after so many years. And the tears came. She didn't miss a Communion service after that unless she was ill. The Lord's Supper was just too precious to her.

The Lord sets the Table

The One who sets the Communion Table already shows its importance. It's Jesus—our loving Savior and best friend, Jesus—the King of kings and Lord of lords. The love behind this meal also shows its importance. It was "on the night he was betrayed" that Jesus instituted his Holy Supper—even while his enemies were pulling death's net tighter around him, his love was preparing a meal that strengthens life. In the looming shadows of

Calvary's cross, he looked at his needy disciples and, in love, left them a wonderful legacy.

And he sets his Table for believers. His gospel net is to be cast out into the world, but his Supper is only for believers. His command that night, "Do this in remembrance of me," was not just for the disciples in the upper room but for believers across the ages. Paul's words to the church at Corinth reinforces this truth: "Whenever you eat this bread and drink this cup, you proclaim the Lord's death until he comes" (1 Corinthians 11:26). Until our loving Lord returns, his meal is there for his disciples to use and enjoy. Unbelievers would hardly be interested. Why would they even want to come to supper with the Lord? For little ones who can't fathom the richness of his Supper and adults who have not been instructed or cannot examine themselves, his Supper is also meaningless. But for those of us who, like Grandma Rebase, know who sets the Table and what he puts on it, this meal is precious beyond words.

The Lord serves rich food

The host sets the menu. For a birthday, cake and ice cream are in order. For Thanksgiving, turkey and pumpkin pie are appropriate. For his Supper, Jesus, as host, also set the menu. And what a rich one it is! Along with bread of flour and fruit of the vine, he offers his true body and blood. Four times he said it—in three of the gospels and one of Paul's epistles: "This *is* my body . . . this *is* my blood." The host of the Supper is the almighty Lord, who knows what he's saying and doing. When he says "is," he means "is." When he says his body is present with the bread and his blood with the wine, he means it and has reasons for saying it. Why do doubting mortals want to change the menu, as if his body and blood are not really present but only symbolized by the bread and wine? Why do others want to claim that the priest changes the bread into his body and the wine into his blood—as if Jesus didn't know what he was saying. In his Supper, Jesus, as host, offers us bread, and along with it, his true body, wine, and along with it, his true blood.

How this miracle happens is incomprehensible for us as his guests, but not impossible for him as our almighty host. Understanding is not what we need, rather believing. As Saint Augustine once wrote: "Understanding is the reward of faith. Therefore, do not seek to understand that you may believe. But believe that you may understand." At his rich Table, the Savior offers what sinners so desperately need. Mere bread and wine would hardly assure them that their sins are forgiven, but his very body, the same body that was broken on the cross in payment for sins, does. So does his very blood, the same blood that stained Calvary's cross in payment for sins. In his Supper, he offers the best there is on earth and in heaven; he offers himself, his body and blood with all his grace. How more convincingly or comfortingly can the sinner be assured of sin's forgiveness than when the Savior comes to him and says: "Here, take, eat my body. It was broken for *you*. Here, drink my blood, it was poured out for *you*."

Those were not tears of sorrow on Grandma Rebase's cheeks that day, but tears of joy. That same joy fills our hearts when Jesus invites us to his Table.

Prayer: "We eat this bread and drink this cup,
       your precious Word believing
       That your true body and your blood
       Our lips are here receiving.
       This Word remains forever true,
       And there is naught you cannot do,
       For you, Lord, are almighty." Amen. (CW 312:4)

Holy Communion

"That is shown us by these words: 'Given' and 'poured out for you for the forgiveness of sins.' Through these words we receive forgiveness of sins, life, and salvation in this sacrament. For where there is forgiveness of sins, there is also life and salvation."

"I need it," said the dying woman from her hospital bed. A sliver of the wafer and a drop of the wine were all her cancerous throat could handle, but oh what they meant for her. "Thank you, pastor," she murmured quietly, and shortly afterward she fell asleep in Jesus' wounds. Certainly we can die without Holy Communion. But what marvelous assurance this sacrament brings us that our God loves us and that all is well between him and us. Such assurance we don't want to reserve just for our dying day, but we want to use it many days in our life.

What blessings the Lord offers in his Supper

We don't come to the Lord's Supper to *do* something for him. When he commanded "Do this in remembrance of me," he wasn't requiring some service of us, something we need to fulfill. Nor was he asking us to come to some church ritual, some tradition that we can take or leave with little loss or gain either way. His words "do this" are more invitation than command. In the Supper we don't go to him, he comes to us. And in his hands, he brings his blessings of "forgiveness of sins, life, and salvation."

Christianity is all about forgiveness of sins. So is the Lord's Supper, as the Savior's words, "Given and poured out for you for the forgiveness of sins," plainly indicate. As the Savior gave his disciples his body and blood together with the bread and wine that Thursday evening, he coupled with them forgiveness of sins. The body and blood he gave his disciples would be given and poured out the next day on the cross in payment for all their sins. With that perfect sacrifice, he would once for all prepare forgiveness for the world's sins. In his Holy Supper, he's at work bringing the blessings of that first Good Friday into the present. With his Supper he assures us that he who died and rose again is right here. His forgiveness is present—as surely as his body that was once given and his blood that was once poured out for sins. Those who have the blessings of forgiveness also have the only life that counts—blessed life with God in heaven and for him on earth. Salvation is theirs, not just in promise but reality. They are redeemed, restored, forgiven, and assured of this blessing by the body and blood of the one who paid for them.

How often might we want to use this blessed Sacrament with its assurance of forgiveness? Like the dying woman in the hospital, let our many daily sins and our ongoing need for forgiveness prompt our answer. And let the knowledge of what rich food his Supper offers bring us there frequently.

What blessings the Lord offers in his Supper to me

When I stand before the Communion Table, Jesus' words "for you" become singular. "For you" becomes "for me." It's for me he suffered and died. It's for me he spreads his Table. That's the appealing beauty of Holy Communion. In the gospel, as the pastor proclaims it,

God's forgiveness is sounded to all. In his Supper he comes to me individually, personally. Those who are with me at his altar are important. They are my brothers and sisters in the faith, standing with me in "common-union" of faith at the altar. But his blessed words "Given and poured out for you for the forgiveness of sins" are for me. I need those words. It's my sins that make me weary and heavy laden. It's my sins that I've lugged with repentance's tears to the altar. I need to feel my Savior's arm around my shoulder and see his loving eyes locked on me as he tells me: "Here, my body, I gave it *for you*. Here, my blood, I poured it out *for you*. *You* can go home in peace."

"I need it," said that dying woman. So do we. Forgiveness of sins is something we can't live or die without. In the hour of trial and temptation, in the times of distress and disappointment, the promise of his forgiveness is our strength and comfort. And in the hour of death, that promise is the pillow on which we can cradle our heads in peace and safety. Thank you, Jesus, for giving your body and pouring out your blood for me!

Prayer: Dear Lord Jesus, thank you for your Supper that was meant for sinners and for your willingness to receive and forgive me. Amen.

Holy Communion

"It is certainly not the eating and drinking that does such things, but the words 'Given' and 'poured out for you for the forgiveness of sins.' These words are the main thing in this sacrament, along with the eating and drinking. And whoever believes these words has what they plainly say, the forgiveness of sins."

"Do you mean it?" we've unfortunately learned to ask. In our day when promises are made, we can't always be sure they'll be kept. People are no longer satisfied with a handshake when deals are put together. Now it takes a printed contract, sometimes in so much legalese that only lawyers can explain it. Even then we can't be one hundred percent sure.

In his Supper our Savior set down his last will and testament for us. He states plainly and, because he did, we can be sure about what he offers us in that blessed meal and how it happens.

His promise offers pardon

Christ offers one clear and simple blessing in his Supper. That blessing is so great that no one can exhaust it. Like some artesian well, it flows perpetually from the Rock of ages all the way to eternity. What might that treasure be? "Forgiveness of sins," Luther reminds us. He also reminds us that this blessing does not come through mere eating and drinking in the sacrament. If it did, if eating and drinking, as some mechanical or semi-magical act, could bring forgiveness, then we might as well eat bread and drink wine more frequently and conveniently in our homes.

It's God Word that connects forgiveness of sins with his sacrament. That's how our gracious God dispenses to sinners the forgiveness he prepared in Christ—through his gospel. With his Supper he connects the specific words "Given and poured out for you for the forgiveness of sins." In these few words lies the whole gospel story. "Given and poured out . . . for the forgiveness of sins" reveals the love that compelled Jesus to die on the cross, consigned him to hell's fury, and carried him into the grave. "For you" reveals his love that reaches for me with all things needful for life and salvation. These are not human words that are not always to be taken at face value. They are divine words, words spoken by one *who means what he says*. Moreover, he can *do* what he says. With his Word he created the world and will one day bring it to judgment. With his Word he healed the sick and will one day raise all the dead. "For the forgiveness of sins" is the sum he writes on this heavenly check with his divine signature on the bottom line. And his check is good!

His promise powers faith

Regardless who approaches his Supper, whether hypocrite or believer, God's promise stands and forgiveness is offered. He is faithful, though others be faithless. All who come receive his body and blood—some for their forgiveness, others for their judgment. The repentant sinner walks away with the tonnage of sin removed from his shoulders. The impenitent leaves with more poundage added, for he "is guilty of sinning against the body and blood of the Lord" (1 Corinthians 11:27). When forgiveness, though offered, is not received, the problem is not with God's loving hand reaching down, but with the hand of the unbelieving recipient.

When Luther wrote "Whoever believes these words has what they plainly say, the forgiveness of sins," he was not indicating that only the strong in faith dare approach. Few, indeed, would be so bold as to come. He was reminding us that the same Spirit who uses the Word to create faith in Baptism uses it also to strengthen faith in the Lord's Supper. His powerful Word does not return empty; it works where and when he determines. Those who come to his Table with his golden words "for your forgiveness" on their hearts, leave with them imprinted even more firmly. Those who approach with the prayer "I do believe; help me overcome my unbelief!" will receive God's answer (Mark 9:24). At the altar, his hand of promise reaching down and our hand of faith created by him are clasped together—his giving and ours receiving.

"Can I be sure?" the crusty farmer asked. He had spent his four score and ten years chasing money, collecting farms, and coming to church just enough to keep the elders off his back. Now he was dying. Hearing his confession in his bedroom, I announced God's forgiveness to him and then offered him the Lord's Supper. But he wanted to be sure. "For you," I reminded him, "Christ gave his body and blood on Calvary for your sins, and now he gives them to you in his Supper. How more sure can we be?" Those who by God's grace believe those blessed words, "for you," will find them changed into "with him" in eternity.

Prayer: "I come, O Savior, to your table,
For weak and weary is my soul;
O Jesus, you alone are able
To satisfy and make me whole.
Lord, may your body and your blood
Be for my soul the highest good!" Amen.

(CW 310:1)

Holy Communion

"Fasting and other outward preparations may serve a good purpose, but he is properly prepared who believes these words: 'Given' and 'poured out for you for the forgiveness of sins.' But whoever does not believe these words or doubts them is not prepared, because the words 'for you' require nothing but hearts that believe."

There's not much fasting these days before going to the Lord's Supper—not like my grandmother who wanted to taste the "best food" first. She knew that refraining from breakfast until after church didn't make her a better communicant, but she used this practice to heighten her appreciation. There's not a lot of dressing up for the Lord's Table either—though I still think that if we dress up for other occasions, we ought to do so even more so for his Supper. There's not even a lot of personal announcing to the pastor a day or two before Communion so that we can give some serious thought to what is coming. Now it's that impersonal card in the entry or in the pew rack to be used on the day of Communion. Changes come and changes go with these outward preparations. But with our inward preparations, some things dare not change if we are to use his Supper with benefit.

Come as a helpless sinner

Attendance at the Lord's Supper is serious business. A Christian knows this and wants to be prepared. He has heard Paul's warning about being guilty of the body and blood of the Lord and doesn't want to receive such precious food to his judgment. He also knows Paul's urging: "A man ought to examine himself before he eats of the bread and drinks of the cup" (1 Corinthians 11:28). So he does, beginning such examination with his heart. He turns to the law, using the Ten Commandments like God's holy fingers pointing to and pressing painfully on his heart. By society's standards many of my sins might appear trivial. There may be no outright murder or adultery, no ending a neighbor's life or enticing away his wife. But by God's standards, my anger and hating, my looking and lusting, my caring for myself at everyone else's, including my God's, expense are just as offensive and intolerable in his sight. And there's nothing I can do, except turn as a helpless sinner to the God of all grace. He has given me a password for entrance into his presence. It's "Lord, have mercy." With this as my plea, I approach his holy Table.

Receive as a penitent believer

Tears of sorrow cannot wash away my guilt. Only one hand can erase the lengthy debit column under my name in God's record book. Only one hand can wipe it clean. That hand has nail prints in it. Jesus stretched those hands out in full payment on the cross for all my sins. In his Supper he now stretches those same hands out to me in comforting assurance with that forgiveness. "This is my body," he says, "believe it." "This is my blood," he says, "believe it." "Given and poured out for the forgiveness of sins," he says, "believe it." "For you," he says, "believe it."

The feet of faith that carry me to his altar may be weak and frail. They may hesitate and falter, but God has promised that when I come in penitent faith, he will not cast me out. When I approach with the penitent sigh "What a wretched man I am! Who will rescue me from this body of death?" he will strengthen faith's grip on the joyous answer: "Thanks be to God—through Jesus Christ our Lord!" (Romans 7:24,25). With this as my confidence, I approach his holy Table.

Leave as an obedient child

"Your sins are forgiven," he says to me in his Supper. As I leave he has something else to say: "Go and sin no more." I cannot approach his Table asking him to leave his fingers off my pet sins. What value is there in such an approach? Nor can I leave his Table without resolving to fight against my sins. What kind of appreciation would that indicate? With sins forgiven and faith strengthened, it's "Lord, help me in the fight against my sins." Though I may not always win the battle, though I may fall even before I leave the church doors, the battle needs to be waged and won more frequently. With this resolve I can leave his holy Table.

Not much fasting these days, not as much dressing up, not nearly as much personal announcing—but coming as a helpless sinner, receiving as a penitent believer, and leaving as his obedient child will always be necessary. Lord, make me into such a worthy communicant!

Prayer: "Grant that we worthily receive
Your supper, Lord, our Savior,
And truly grieving for our sins,
May prove by our behavior
That we are thankful for your grace
And day by day may run our race,
In holiness increasing." Amen (CW 312:7)